CROWN THEOLOGICAL LIBRARY

VOL. XIV.
BOUSSET'S JESUS

Crown Theological Library

WORKS ALREADY PUBLISHED

Vol. I.—BABEL AND BIBLE. By Dr FRIEDRICH DELITZSCH. 5s.

Vol. II.—THE VIRGIN BIRTH OF CHRIST. An Historical and Critical Essay. By PAUL LOBSTEIN. 3s.

Vol. III.—MY STRUGGLE FOR LIGHT. Confessions of a Preacher. By R. WIMMER. 3s. 6d.

Vol. IV.—LIBERAL CHRISTIANITY. Its Origin, Nature, and Mission. By JEAN RÉVILLE. 4s.

Vol. V.—WHAT IS CHRISTIANITY? By ADOLF HARNACK. 5s.

Vol. VI.—FAITH AND MORALS. By W. HERRMANN. 5s.

Vol. VII.—EARLY HEBREW STORY. A Study of the Origin, the Value, and the Historical Background of the Legends of Israel. By JOHN P. PETERS, D.D. 5s.

Vol. VIII.—BIBLE PROBLEMS AND THE NEW MATERIAL FOR THEIR SOLUTION. By Prof. T. K. CHEYNE, D.Litt., D.D. 5s.

Vol. IX.—THE DOCTRINE OF THE ATONEMENT AND ITS HISTORICAL EVOLUTION, AND RELIGION AND MODERN CULTURE. By the late AUGUSTE SABATIER. 4s. 6d.

Vol. X.—THE EARLY CHRISTIAN CONCEPTION OF CHRIST: its Significance and Value in the History of Religion. By OTTO PFLEIDERER. 3s. 6d.

Vol. XI.—THE CHILD AND RELIGION. Eleven Essays by Various Writers. 6s.

Vol. XII.—THE EVOLUTION OF RELIGION: An Anthropological Study. By L. R. FARNELL, M.A., D.Litt. 5s.

Vol. XIII.—THE HISTORY OF EARLY CHRISTIAN LITERATURE. The Books of the New Testament. By Baron H. VON SODEN. 5s.

JESUS

BY

W. BOUSSET
PROFESSOR OF THEOLOGY AT THE UNIVERSITY OF GÖTTINGEN

TRANSLATED BY
JANET PENROSE TREVELYAN

EDITED BY
Rev. W. D. MORRISON, LL.D.

Wipf and Stock Publishers
EUGENE, OREGON

Wipf and Stock Publishers
199 West 8th Avenue, Suite 3
Eugene, Oregon 97401

Jesus
By Bousset, W.
ISBN: 1-59244-173-4
Publication date: March, 2003
Previously published by Williams & Norgate, January, 1906.

CONTENTS

BOOK I

THE OUTWARD COURSE OF THE LIFE OF JESUS, AND THE FORMS OF HIS ACTIVITY

	PAGES
CHAPTER I. THE MINISTRY	1–18
CHAPTER II. THE CHARACTER OF JESUS, AND HIS RELATIONS WITH CONTEMPORARY RABBINISM AND ESSENISM	19–35
CHAPTER III. JESUS AS PREACHER AND HEALER	36–58
CHAPTER IV. DISCIPLES AND OPPONENTS	59–70

BOOK II

THE TEACHING OF JESUS

CHAPTER V. THE KINGDOM OF GOD	71–98
CHAPTER VI. JESUS' CONCEPTION OF GOD	99–116
CHAPTER VII. THE LAST JUDGMENT	117–129
CHAPTER VIII. THE MORAL TEACHING OF JESUS	130–165

BOOK III

THE MYSTERY OF THE PERSON

		PAGES
CHAPTER IX.	JESUS AND THE MESSIAHSHIP	166–180
CHAPTER X.	THE SON OF MAN	181–194
CHAPTER XI.	CONCLUSION	195–211

JESUS

BOOK I

THE OUTWARD COURSE OF THE LIFE OF JESUS, AND THE FORMS OF HIS ACTIVITY

CHAPTER I

The Ministry

ONE small section of the life of Jesus, the short period of his public activity, is all that our authorities allow us to survey. Its beginnings lie plunged in darkness. The accounts given by Matthew and Luke in the first chapters of their Gospels belong to the domain of legend, as is shown by the fact that our earliest Gospel knows nothing of any such events, while even the fourth passes them over in silence. Nor do the reports of these two Gospels agree in any point, except in the single statement that Jesus was born at Bethlehem. And even here a considerable discrepancy appears. With Luke the better historical tradition that Nazareth was in reality Jesus' native town still makes itself felt; and according to his account, therefore, Jesus was born in Bethlehem in consequence of his parents' journey thither to be enrolled in the census of Augustus. Matthew, on the other hand, assumes as self-evident that Jesus' parents originally lived in Bethlehem, and gives express reasons for their migration to Nazareth a few years later. The two accounts are absolutely contradictory, and represent two separate attempts at reconciling the older tradition that Nazareth was Jesus' birthplace with the later assumption that, as Messiah, he must have been born at Bethlehem. Nor is it possible, by rejecting Matthew's report, to save that of Luke, on the plea that the latter is simpler and fresher than Matthew's dogmatic structure, with its framework of Old Testament prophecies. For the story which Luke

The Ministry

takes as the very core of his narrative—the census under Augustus and the journey of Jesus' parents to Bethlehem—is full of historical impossibilities. And, above all, the central point of both accounts is formed by the story of the miraculous birth, which betrays itself by its very content to be a piece of dogmatic legend. It is ignored by our Gospels in the actual body of their narratives, *e.g.* when they speak without reserve of Jesus' *brothers and sisters*,[1] and of himself as the carpenter's son; or still more when they record that Mary, his mother, once came seeking to fetch her son home, because she thought he was beside himself.[2] Paul not only knows nothing of this dogma, but witnesses against it when he speaks of Jesus as "of the seed of David according to the flesh,"[3] or when, in a passage in which he is emphasising the fact that in order to redeem us Jesus Christ became in all respects like unto us, he speaks of him as "born of a woman."[4] Finally, a

[1] Mark vi. 3.   [2] Mark iii. 21 and 32.
[3] Rom. i. 3.   [4] Gal. iv. 4.

direct contradiction to the idea of the miraculous birth is formed by the genealogies both in Matthew and Luke,[1] in which Jesus' descent from David is proved by reference to the Davidic origin of *Joseph*. They must have arisen before the appearance of the birth-stories, for through them they lose all meaning and all object. And it happens that, in a recently discovered manuscript of an early Syriac translation, we find Matthew's genealogy actually ending with the words: "Joseph, to whom Mary the Virgin was betrothed, begat Jesus, who is called Messiah."

That our faith loses nothing by the abandonment of the dogma of the miraculous birth is best shown in the person and piety of Paul the Apostle. No man's faith in Jesus Christ could have been more fervent, more glowing than his; yet he knew nothing of the miraculous birth. The mystery of the person of Jesus does not lie in the manner of its outward origin. Nor will the first chapters of Luke,

[1] Matt. i. 1–6; Luke iii. 23–38.

The Ministry

with their wonderful poetic beauty, ever cease to be full of meaning and value for us, even though we regard them as pure legend. They bear within themselves their value for all time. They are the glittering halo which the poetic faith of the first community set upon the head of Jesus. The forms of that faith are transitory, but the faith itself in its inmost essence still remains: "I bring you tidings of great joy, for there is born to you this day a Saviour." Luke must ever be to us the writer of the Christmas gospel, whether we take his narrative as literal truth or as poetic fairy-tale.

Our acquaintance with Jesus begins only when he has attained the prime of manhood, at the age of about thirty, and is entering upon his career of public activity. His appearance is intimately connected, according to our tradition, with that of another great emissary of the Lord to the people of Israel—John the Baptist. Now who was John the Baptist? All things considered, we can say, in Jesus' own words, that he was a prophet.[1] After centuries of drought in the religious life of the people, here at last was an apparition on the old grand scale. A prophet after the manner of the great prophets of old, he preached repentance and judgment, and sought to free his countrymen from their ancient deep-rooted madness of self-complacency and self-assurance: "Begin not to say within yourselves, 'We have Abraham to our father': for I say unto you that God is able of these stones to raise up children unto Abraham."[2] In two respects the figure of John the Baptist eclipses that of the ancient prophets and assumes a new and special character. With none of them did *asceticism* play so great a part as with him. He made his appearance in the desert, clad in the scanty clothing of the desert-dwellers, and eating the desert food. The business of everyday life was hateful to him; he constrained his hearers to come out into the wilderness, that in the

[1] Matt. xi. 9.   [2] Luke iii. 8.

stillness of dead nature they might find their God, whom they had lost among men. But in addition, John was the originator of a remarkable novelty—the external religious rite of *baptism*. What was the true meaning of the baptism of John we are now scarcely in a position to say. In any case, both he and his hearers attached great importance to it, and he was known as the Baptist on account of it. It was the tribute paid by the great John to the later national piety, now nearing its decay and inclined to lay an ever-increasing stress upon external rites and ceremonies of a sacred or miraculous nature.

That Jesus was directly indicated by John as Messiah, as the Christian tradition has it, we do not believe. John prophesied a Messiah who should come with his winnowing-fan in his hand and with fire from heaven.[1] The appearance of Jesus was altogether different from that of the Messiah whom John expected. It was only when John lay in prison that the

[1] Matt. iii. 11, 12.

belief dawned in his soul that this might be " He that cometh," the Messiah.[1] But indirectly his preaching was of great importance to the entry of Jesus upon the scene. He prepared the way for Jesus' activity. The movement which he had called forth was still agitating the souls of the people with its long after-swell when Jesus began his ministry.

It is part of the most trustworthy substance of our tradition that Jesus went to be baptized by John the Baptist. The fact that the Christian community objected very early to the idea that the Sinless One should have accepted the baptism of the forgiveness of sins,[2] makes it impossible that its members should ever have invented this incident in the life of Jesus. Further, a tradition which we have no reason to distrust, tells us that at his baptism Jesus had an experience, a vision, which was the turning-point in his life. He saw the heavens opened and heard the voice

---

[1] Matt. xi. 2 ff.
[2] Matt. iii. 14 f. is an attempt to remove the objection.

of God ring through his soul: "Thou art my Son."[1] Nor is it psychologically improbable that after this momentous event the hour of temptation should have come upon him.[2] After the divine voice had filled his whole being with its mighty sound, the earthly nature rose up against it and must needs be fought down to the bitter end.

Thus had Jesus ripened and matured for his appearance in public. As to the time and place of that event, we are not wholly without information. Luke tells us that the preaching of John took place in the fifteenth year of the reign of Tiberius Cæsar,[3] *i.e.* between the 19th of August 28 and the 19th of August 29; and since John's career must to all appearance have been very short, the date of Jesus' baptism and of the beginning of his ministry cannot be placed at too great a distance from it. According to the Gospel of Luke, he was at that time "about" thirty years of age.[4] If,

---

[1] Mark i. 9–11. [2] Mark i. 12–13.
[3] Luke iii. 1. [4] Luke iii. 23.

as it seems, we are right in assuming that Jesus was born before the death of Herod the Great,[1] he was actually a little more than thirty at the time of his first appearance, for Herod died in the year 4 B.C.; but, on the other hand, we are compelled to assign his birth to the very end of the reign of Herod. Judæa was now under the direct rule of the Romans, after the deposition and banishment in 6 A.D. of Archelaus, son of Herod the Great. Pontius Pilate held the office of procurator (26–36 A.D.), and under him the Jewish high priest (at this time Caiaphas, 17–35 A.D.), held a position of some independence. Galilee was still ruled by a son of Herod the Great, Antipas, by whom the Baptist was imprisoned and executed. Jesus entered on his ministry not in his own home, the little inland hill-town of Nazareth, lying on the southern slope of Galilee, but in Capernaum, a city standing in a narrow plain on the western shore of the

---

[1] Luke i. 5, and *cf.* the account, though a legendary one, in Matt. ii. 1 ff.

The Ministry

Lake of Galilee, shut in on the west by a mountain ridge. In the first chapter of Mark,[1] a vivid picture has survived of his first day's preaching at Capernaum.

We know nothing definite as to the duration of Jesus' ministry. The narrative of our first three Evangelists is timeless. Even if their report is accurate, we are not justified in concluding from the fact that they record but one journey of Jesus to Jerusalem, that his activity lasted but a single year. On the other hand, the chronology of the fourth Gospel, with its division of Jesus' life according to the Jewish feasts, is not above suspicion, and cannot be accepted as it stands. Still, we cannot assume too long a duration for the ministry. Jesus' death must be placed not long after the year 30, since, according to the fairly unanimous conclusion of investigators, the conversion of Paul took place at latest in the middle of the thirties.

We are no longer in a position to reconstruct

[1] i. 16–39.

an historical picture of the ministry of Jesus in Galilee according to its chronological development, for the narrative of our Gospels, with its prevailing timelessness and its frequent arrangement of the words and deeds of Jesus in a designedly material order, does not provide the means necessary for such a picture. Only a few scanty data can be established with certainty: that his success and the enthusiasm of the multitude steadily increased at first; that he gradually gathered round him a band of disciples and followers whose devotion was unbounded, but that then a gradual slackening of enthusiasm set in, and that towards the end of his Galilean ministry he saw himself surrounded by dangers, which he sought to avoid by a considerable journey towards the north; that his following grew less and less, and that he deliberately restricted himself to the instruction of his own disciples. The little that does introduce some movement into the record of his life we are left to read between the lines of the Gospels, rather than that they

The Ministry

definitely state it; and the question is, whether the inquirers into the life of Jesus have always been right in their readings. A few separate scenes recorded by the Evangelists seem to have been of special importance to the internal course of his life and teaching, such as, above all, the solemn confession at Cæsarea Philippi, when Peter answered the Master's question, "Who say ye that I am?" with the unhesitating words: "Thou art the Christ."[1] Here it certainly seems as though Jesus were speaking to his disciples for the first time (and probably towards the end of his ministry) of the Messianic secret of his person, and as though the confession of the disciples were also made now for the first time. But our Evangelists leave us to guess this, while they themselves pass quickly over the scene without expressing themselves in any way as to its inward meaning. Further, it seems probable that Jesus did not speak to his disciples of his approaching suffering and death until towards

[1] Mark viii. 27 ff.

the end of his life; and nothing is more natural and indeed more necessary than to suppose that the thought of death arose but slowly in his mind, in connection with those bitter and disappointing experiences at the hands of the people, which we are left to conclude from his stern judgments upon them. But again, our Gospels do not state this explicitly, nay, they even make Jesus speak of his suffering and death at the very beginning of his ministry.[1]

In short, wherever it is a question of the internal course of Jesus' life, we find ourselves plunged in uncertainties and obliged to be content with conjectures of a greater or less degree of probability. On the whole, his life and teaching flowed on in an even course, without any strong outward signs of development, in the grand and simple channels which he had chosen from the beginning. Wandering from place to place, preaching, healing, comforting sinners, attacking the leaders of the people, gathering a band of

[1] Mark ii. 20.

The Ministry

disciples, Jesus passed through the cities and villages of Galilee, until his time was fulfilled.

Then at the end of his life he journeyed up to Jerusalem—probably for the first time since the beginning of his ministry proper. Here also we do not really learn the reason for the step. The explanation apparently given by the Gospels is that he went up to Jerusalem to meet his death. Yet the scene in Gethsemane argues against this view, for it shows plainly that to the last he had admitted the possibility that the doom of death might pass him by. We may probably assume that Jesus journeyed to Jerusalem under the dim impulse and consciousness that there his destiny would be accomplished, in the manner ordained him by his Father.

From this point onward our records become fuller; indeed they follow the events of the life of Jesus almost from day to day. A series of well-attested and internally connected incidents pass before our eyes: the Messianic entry into Jerusalem, the cleansing of the temple, the betrayal of Judas, the last supper with the disciples, Gethsemane and the arrest, the trial before the high priest, with Jesus' confession to the Messiahship,[1] the denial of Peter, the judgment before Pilate, the death of Jesus on the cross. The scenes follow one another with catastrophic swiftness, and on the whole we obtain a good general view. Here too, however, we often seek in vain for some insight into the course of events below the surface. We should give much to know where to look for the forces at work behind the catastrophe; for Jesus' old opponents, the Scribes and Pharisees, have now disappeared from the scene. In their place the Jerusalemic authorities—high priest and council—stand out as the arch-foes. But what was the cause of so swift a growth of enmity in these new

[1] This scene, in spite of all objections recently raised against it (*e.g.* by W. Brandt in his *Geschichte Jesu*) has a kernel of historic truth. We cannot measure the tumultuous proceedings against Jesus by the standards of the regular procedure of the Jewish tribunals known to us from later sources.

The Ministry

opponents? Where are the obscure motive forces to be sought? And what was the part played in the trial by the Roman authorities, by Pilate? Our Gospels are evidently anxious to throw all the blame upon the Jews, and to represent the Roman governor as half on the side of Jesus, and only borne along by the unruly proceedings of his accusers against his own better judgment. But the question has quite rightly been raised, whether Pontius Pilate's share in the trial of Jesus, as it is represented in our Gospels, is really consistent with the character of this extremely harsh and bloody governor, to whom a few executions more or less would be a matter of no importance; and whether the Romans did not perhaps play a far more active part in the condemnation of Jesus. But whether his chief accusers were Jews or Gentiles, or a combination of both, it is at any rate certain that Jesus was condemned to death as Messiah and because of his Messianic claims. That Pilate ordered the words, "This is the King of the

Jews,"[1] to be inscribed on the cross, is a piece of good evangelic tradition.

Finally, we know that Jesus was put to death on a Friday. But our Gospel witnesses differ even as to the date of the fatal day. It appears certain that our first three Gospels represent Jesus as suffering crucifixion on the 15th of Nizan,[2] while the fourth makes it the 14th.[3] No unanimity has yet been reached among scholars on the question which of these two dates is the correct one; but even among those who usually look upon the Johannine tradition with the greatest suspicion, there is now a considerable tendency to give the preference to it in this one instance. The attempts to ascertain the year and month of Jesus' death by astronomical means, *i.e.* by calculating in which of the years about 30 the 14th or 15th of Nizan fell on a Friday, have as yet led to no perfectly definite result.

[1] Mark xv. 26.
[2] According to Mark xiv. 12, the arrest took place on the evening of the 14th of Nizan.
[3] John xiii. 1; xviii. 28; xix. 31.

CHAPTER II

The Character of Jesus, and his Relations with contemporary Rabbinism and Essenism

OUR knowledge of Jesus is very small if we approach our authorities with the desire to reconstruct the life, or, as we now prefer to call it, the history of Jesus, according to its development and its inward connecting links. We soon find ourselves lost in a maze of uncertainties and conjectures.

It will be well, therefore, to forego all attempts at a formal life or history of Jesus. Yet our knowledge of him is far greater than the preceding scanty survey would lead us to suppose. We have only to strike out the right path, and to ask our questions in the right way. If we are not in a position to form a connected picture of the course of Jesus' career, we can yet realise his figure, thrown out, as it were, against a flat background; for the figure of Jesus is so simple and on such grand lines, it stands out so complete and so mature from the first hour of his activity to the last, that it bears the test of being represented in stationary relief, and does not become lifeless even when deprived of the clearness lent by a presentation based on development.

In our attempt at reconstruction we shall proceed from the outer to the inner, and shall begin with a sketch of the unchanging external forms in which the life and activity of Jesus in Galilee were cast. We shall ask ourselves in what general manner Jesus set about his task, with what express aims and objects and by what means he sought to influence his hearers, who were his opponents, where he found his adherents, and how he behaved towards his friends. And in this way we shall soon find that we obtain a most vivid and striking picture of his ministry.

The Character of Jesus

In considering Jesus' mission as a whole, it may best be called a prophetic one. It was not in any sense expressly Messianic, as we shall point out more clearly below. Perhaps it was not until his entry into Jerusalem that Jesus proclaimed himself to the multitude as Messiah; certainly it was not until the end of his sojourn in Galilee that he set his disciples the Messianic question. To the people he was "one of the prophets,"[1] or else they placed him on a level with John the Baptist;[2] their verdict was, "He speaks as one that hath authority (*i.e.* as a prophet), and not as the Scribes."[3] Jesus once spoke of himself and John the Baptist together as the children of wisdom.[4] And indeed we must go back to the great prophets of the Old Testament before we find figures on anything approaching the scale of the Baptist and Jesus. Only with them do we come upon the same power of popular speech, the same dreadful earnest in

[1] Mark viii. 28.   [2] Matt. xi. 28.
[3] Mark i. 22.   [4] Luke vii. 35.

the preaching of judgment to come, the same ardour in the struggle against the powers that be and the idle masses, the same insistence upon inwardness and truth in worship, the same grand art of standing alone.

And yet there are certain differences between the manner of Jesus and that of the ancient prophets. If the Baptist differed from their example in one direction,[1] Jesus differed in another. The figure of the Baptist is more ascetic and anti-worldly, harsher and more impassioned, than theirs, while the figure of Jesus is more human and accessible, and breathes a greater sense of harmony and peace.

Nevertheless we ought not to lay too great a stress upon this side of Jesus' character. We run some danger of painting him in colours too harmonious and peaceful. It is only recently that we have begun to pay more attention to the other side of the picture, and have asked ourselves whether Jesus was not a

[1] See p. 6 above.

The Character of Jesus 23

visionary, whether he did not live a large part of his life in regions beyond those of ordinary consciousness. We must not forget that once during his ministry his mother and his brethren came to fetch him home, thinking he was "beside himself,"[1] and that his opponents charged him with working his cures by the power of an evil spirit, Beelzebub.[2] Experiences of a visionary nature are, moreover, to be found in his life, though they are not very frequent. According to the Gospel tradition, his baptismal vision at the outset of his ministry brought him to a final decision concerning himself and his task. And after it, as our Gospels relate, the Spirit drove him into the wilderness, where he was tempted of the devil. Once he himself tells his disciples that he had beheld Satan "fallen as lightning from heaven."[3] If we can trust the reports of the transfiguration given by our Gospels, he even included his disciples in his other-worldly experiences. Nor must we forget his agony

[1] Mark iii. 21, 35.   [2] Mark iii. 22.   [3] Luke x. 18.

of prayer in Gethsemane, when, as Luke tells us, he wrestled so earnestly that the sweat stood out upon his forehead like drops of blood, nor his repeated flights into the wilderness, nor the violent agitations of soul which seized him, especially when healing or performing his "mighty works," nor his sudden outbursts of wrath, nor the many incidents in his life in which he seems to be acting under the influence of some obscure, inexplicable storm and stress,[1] nor the overmastering force with which he made his strangely severe moral demands, nor the ardent confidence with which he announced the nearness of the wonderful Kingdom. Indeed it could not have been otherwise. We must realise the fact once for all, that the life of the greatest in God's Kingdom does not move in the sober light of every day, but that a large part of it lies in regions to us mysterious and unfamiliar. Fearful and irresistible forces rule in its depths, vast possibilities arise, a new

[1] Mark i. 35, 38; vi. 31, 45; x. 32.

world stirs within it and strives towards the surface with the pangs of travail. The devil and his demons wrestle with the angels of God, mortal despair alternates with a heavenly confidence of victory, night struggles with day, the clouds descend, but between their rifts are seen the rays of the brightening stars. Then when a flash from this innermost life touches our souls, when its depths are stirred and rise up with volcanic force, we stand amazed and begin dimly to conceive the terrible inward greatness of such a soul-life. So it was with Jesus.

Yet the reverse side of that life was greater still. As Paul once said, "Whether we are beside ourselves, it is unto God; or whether we are of sober mind, it is unto you,"[1] and there lies the great secret of the moral force of Jesus' life. Again and again he knew how to curb the mighty forces that wrestled within his soul for the benefit of his fellow-men. If he yearned to kindle a consuming fire, he

[1] 2 Cor. v. 13.

knew also what its destructive power would be; he could forbear, and he laid no impossible or unnecessary burdens on the souls of his disciples. The burdens which must needs be borne after the parting of the ways to which he brought his followers were heavy enough. Thus it happens that the impression of calmness and certainty, of kindness, peace, and spiritual harmony is still the strongest in our total picture of Jesus. When we compare his personality with that of Paul, his life with that of the earliest Christian community, it is astonishing how little we hear in it of "the Spirit," that bringer of all the stormy, supernatural excitements and the miraculous powers of the first community-life. The visionary element likewise plays but a small part in the reports of our Gospels. Of Jesus' wrestlings in the wilderness we are told practically nothing—merely the bare fact that he went into the wilderness. In short, we are left with the idea that a far mightier storm and stress was at work in his soul than he ever

The Character of Jesus

allowed to penetrate to the surface. It is significant that the multitude clearly grasped the difference in this respect between Jesus and the Baptist. Whereas the Baptist gave the impression of a man possessed by a higher power, Jesus appeared by comparison as an ordinary, everyday person: "Behold a gluttonous man and a wine-bibber, a friend of publicans and sinners."[1] It is when we contrast these two figures that, beside the agitated and stormful presence of the Baptist, the personality of Jesus stands out in greater simplicity, measure, and harmony, and with a kindlier inclination towards the workaday life of men.

Even when we compare Jesus with the prophets of the Old Testament, the same difference becomes apparent. In contrast with them, how homely, how true to human life, is the figure of Jesus! Where among those dark, tremendous personages do we find features so sunny or so purely human as with

[1] Matt. xi. 19.

Jesus? Where do we read of a prophet who called the children to him in the street and fondled them? Jesus' heart warmed to the children, to the sunshine in their eyes and the magic of the spring in their hearts, no less than to the birds of the air and the flowers of the field; he loved to go down into the quiet and happiness of the people's homes; he would let Martha go busily about her household work while Mary sat listening at his feet, and he rejoiced with the joyous at weddings and festivals. The prophets moved along the lofty walks of life, amid world-famous events, the struggles of the great, and the intrigues of palaces; they were the counsellors of kings, and lived far removed from the multitude. Jesus, on the other hand, spent his life among common men, in the midst of the crowd, in constant intercourse with the lower strata of the people, mixing with simple folk in all their everyday aspects; and hence the charm of infinite wealth and infinite many-sidedness encircles him.

The Character of Jesus

Yet we must not forget that both sides of the character of Jesus were fused in one. However ordinary the circumstances, Jesus himself is never ordinary. Like the sun, which sheds its gentle warmth upon the earth and yet remains the sun, clothed in unique beauty, overwhelming force and raging heat, the least part of which would suffice to consume the life it created, so does Jesus appear among his surroundings. When we look deeper into his life, we see both the mighty motive forces below the surface and the heroic moral strength with which they were held down. This indeed is where we find him greatest—in his restrained strength, his pent-up wealth, his calmness in the midst of storm, the harmony he produces from the most jarring discords.

When we examine the personal activity of Jesus more closely, in the light of the forms it borrowed from his times, it can be said that he added to the prophetic manner—which was the deepest note of his being—something of the best in the rabbinic learning of his day. Strange as it may sound, it is nevertheless true that Jesus bears some resemblance to his bitterest opponents in the manner of his teaching. Even a superficial glance shows much that is akin. His preaching in the synagogue, his disputations and expounding of the Scriptures, his wandering from place to place and gathering of disciples—these were also the principal forms in which the lives of the famous Rabbis of his day were cast. Even his practice of healing and casting out of devils can be traced among them. And we shall see later on that he owed the vehicle on which he mainly relied in his popular preaching—the parable—more particularly to the synagogue and the Scribes. As the Rabbis taught their disciples first and foremost how to pray, so Jesus' disciples came to him with the petition, "Lord, teach us to pray."[1] Like the Rabbis, Jesus is addressed by his disciples and followers as "Lord," "Rabbi," "Master,"

[1] Luke xi. 1.

"Teacher." As they were frequently supported by their pupils—although this was not the rule, and many regulations existed against it, exhorting them to live on the produce of their labour and to teach the law for nothing—so Jesus, and even his disciples too, depended for their support on the resources of their followers.

But his connections with rabbinism were not of an external or even antagonistic nature only; rather the web of his teaching is crossed and recrossed with spiritual threads from the rabbinic woof. Moreover, a new and not strictly prophetic element associated with his ordinary manner—the pedagogic—originates with them. Some writers have thought it necessary to dispute the pedagogic element in Jesus altogether, in favour of his intuitive, prophetic manner. And indeed there is no doubt that too much stress has often been laid on the calmly instructive and edifying side of Jesus' personality. Certainly he was no ordinary sort of pedagogue, and pedagogy was not all in all to him. He was never known to suppress a truth or to make present sacrifice of a final end for pedagogic reasons. He wished to cast fire upon the earth, "and would that it were already kindled!"[1] He did not gradually lift his disciples to higher levels, but set them immediately before a stern alternative; he was more inclined to repel the multitude than to sue for its favour;[2] he did not argue with his opponents: he annihilated them. The spirit that would "compass sea and land to make one proselyte,"[3] with all its equivocations and compromises, he utterly abhorred. He could speak harsh, biting words, which were apt to offend and wound his hearers, and the meaning of which was only to be won by hard mental effort; and he was fond of exhibiting things in all their forbidding harshness, one-sidedness, and crudity. Who can reproach him for it? A prophet cannot always be a pedagogue as well. Yet when all

[1] Luke xii. 50. (The above is a literal translation of the German version.—TRANS.)

[2] Luke xiv. 25 ff.

[3] Matt. xxiii. 15.

Relations with Essenism

is said and done, Jesus *was* a pedagogue within the limits set him by his prophetic calling. We have only to remember how large a part was played in his public ministry by plain, homely teaching, and how in his parables he cares only for what is simple, clear, and didactic. Where among the prophets of the Old Testament does the personal intercourse with the disciples, the gradual pouring out of the riches of the soul into the souls of others, play so great a part as with Jesus? The work of the prophets ended with their lives, or at most the memory and influence of the Master was kept alive for a short time by a few followers. But when Jesus was no more, a band of disciples remained, ready and able to carry on the great work of their Master with energy and courage.

Attempts have often been made to establish a relation between Jesus and the remarkable society of pietists who are known under the name of Essenes, and who enjoyed a very high consideration at the time of which we are speaking. Like them, it is urged, Jesus forbade the swearing of oaths. Starting from this fact, it is sought to prove that Jesus devoted all his energies to the gathering of disciples, and that he founded an order in the manner of the Essenic order, while above all the absolute prohibition laid upon the inner circle of his disciples to possess property is adduced as a parallel. We must, however, entirely reject any proposal to establish a connection between them. Jesus had nothing whatever to do with the sect of the Essenes. Essenism was an anti-worldly monachism, and its chief features were an intense exclusiveness, a withdrawal from the world, and a renunciation of all active effect upon it. What part or lot had Jesus with those strange anchorites who made it a rule that, if one of their number happened to meet any person not belonging to the order, or even an initiated novice, he must immediately take a cleansing bath, because he had defiled himself! What was there in common between Jesus' eager desire to work while he had the light, between his

Relations with Essenism

joy in labour, and the cloister-like retirement of the Essenic sect? There is, moreover, yet another consideration. The Essenic order was a sacramental community, and the main features of its pietism consisted in mystic rites, consecrations, bathings, and common meals of a sacrificial nature. Now Jesus is absolutely free from such tendencies; everything in his teaching is directed towards the spiritual and the personal. He did not baptize as John had done; the Christian baptism was the creation of the community he left behind him. And if, on the last evening of his life, he gave his disciples bread and wine as his body and blood, it is most improbable that he meant thereby to institute a regular rite.[1] Whatever his exact object was in gathering his band of disciples, he certainly did not intend thereby to create a monastic order. The difference is complete both in form and in spiritual content, and the few superficial resemblances which do exist cannot possibly affect this judgment.

[1] See below, p. 109.

CHAPTER III

Jesus as Preacher and Healer

THE greater part of Jesus' activity was spent in teaching and preaching. His first appearance in Galilee was made as a popular preacher. Any place would serve his purpose. He would often use the synagogue, but did not, like the Scribes, confine himself to it. Rather he preached in the streets and squares, in the houses themselves and in the open air, on the slope of a mountain or from a boat on the lake. Only the rabbinic schools and their disputations—if indeed these played any part at all in Galilee—he entirely avoided. And wherever he appeared, the multitude crowded round the wonderful man, pouring in from afar and following him for many a league.

He had but to show himself, and the people came; when he went into the wilderness, multitudes followed in his train.

Now, wherein lay the strange and mysterious power of his discourse? Its form we may regard as a mixture between the early prophets' preaching of repentance and the mode of teaching adopted by the Scribes. Jesus combined the best points of both. From the former he took its fire and energy, its earnestness, and its insistence upon essentials; from the latter the calmer didactic tone, the "pedagogic" element, the wealth and variety of treatment, the attention paid to the everyday questions of religious and moral life. Yet what the people were mainly conscious of was the *difference* between his manner and the accustomed ways of their former teachers: "He speaks as one that hath authority, and not as the Scribes." What they heard from the Scribes was in truth but Scripture-learning. Everything turned upon the letter of the law and its exegesis. The merely legal and ceremonial side, with its mass of ordinances, occupied by far the largest space in it. Much that was good and useful for religion and morals was no doubt let fall by the way, but only by the way—it could not be enjoyed to the full. Trained acumen, a system of explaining separate passages of Scripture by the most artificial rules, idle, fantastic combinations, devices of greater or less ingenuity, punning interpretations and burlesque anecdotes—these were the characteristics of the rabbinic discourses. Jesus' attitude towards the Scriptures was in theory no other than that of his contemporaries. He too bowed to the authority of that which was "written," usually with unqualified homage, and again and again he proved his point, especially in arguing with opponents, by appealing to the letter of the Scriptures.[1] But with him the Scriptures and the law were never an end in themselves, but only a means to an end; his

[1] Mark xii. 26 ff.; xii. 36.

business was, not to expound the Scriptures, but to lead men to the living God. Whatever he could make use of for that purpose he took from the Scriptures; whatever was useless simply glanced aside from his largeness of soul and his devotion to the real. Certainly the Scriptures had authority for him, but when there was no other way he would sometimes, if only half-consciously, break through its limits; and in that case he was fond of setting passage against passage, authority against authority.[1] But just as he saw authority in the Scriptures, so he submitted with equal earnestness and humility to the laws of God as he read them in nature and in the life of man.

Here, then, lay the difference. The message he brought was a living reality, not a clinging to the skirts of a vanished world; it was religion here and now. *He himself* had something to say; he himself, his own person with its inexhaustible mines of wealth, was to be

[1] Mark x. 1 ff.

found in his discourses. The message he brought was the living God, with His goodness and faithfulness, His deep, holy will and His gracious promises. Here was no place for conceits and word-plays, here was no straining after effect; what Jesus brought was soul-refreshing earnestness and intense keenness of purpose, never an idle drifting into futile cleverness.

Being so much in earnest with the matter, he had the manner at command in an unique degree. Let us take a somewhat closer view of the forms which he employed. Their characteristic feature is universally felt to be the parable. Among the sayings of Jesus which have come down to us, the parables take the first place both in bulk and in importance. But even where his discourse does not take the form of the connected parable, it is studded with similes and images. The Gospels themselves lay stress on his "speaking in parables." The word parable (maschal) was used at that time to denote all the various forms of pictorial and even of enigmatical speech, and included the parable proper, the strictly didactic simile, the riddle and the "dark saying," the form which we should call paradox,[1] the fable, the symbolising narrative, and the allegory. That from among all these forms Jesus selected one—the didactic parable—almost exclusively, is a sign of his deepest nature, for his parables almost always served an eminently practical purpose. His desire was to teach, not to ask riddles or to make ingenious puns and witticisms in order to arouse a superficial interest. And he attains his purpose by means of the simile. When he wishes to bring home to his hearers some divine idea that he has to proclaim, he tells a simple story of everyday life, or dwells on some process of nature familiar to his audience. He leaves them to discover the idea behind the parable, which is always simple and easy to deduce. Thus

[1] In Mark vii. 17 a saying of Jesus is termed *parabolé* (maschal), where we should actually use the word *paradox*.

the parable becomes the bridge by which he leads his hearers out of the world of familiar, trivial occurrences into the eternal world of God and God's thought, out of the realm of nature into the realm of the spirit. A moment ago they were still there; now with but slight effort they have made the crossing. Jesus takes his hearers as they are, plain men and women toiling in the common dust and fulfilling their everyday tasks,—but in the midst of this life of theirs, in the midst of the world they know so well, he makes the great thoughts of God flash into their ken. Nothing could be more preposterous than the statement of Mark,[1] and following him of the other Evangelists, that Jesus spoke in parables in order that the hearts of the people should be hardened. That is the dogmatic pedantry of a later age, which serves no purpose and only obscures the clear image of Jesus. It is amply contradicted by his unmistakable tone throughout the parables.

[1] Mark iv. 11 ff.

This form of address Jesus likewise owed to the rabbinic learning of his day. There can be no doubt that he first learnt such a manner of teaching in the synagogue. All that has come down to us in the way of parables from the rabbinic tradition—later though they undoubtedly are—bears so close a resemblance both in form and matter to the parables of Jesus, that no idea of accident can be entertained. And since any influence of Jesus upon the later Jewish rabbinism is out of the question, we can only assume that Jesus had caught the form of his parabolic speech from the Scribes in the synagogue. This is not in any sense to disparage him. For it is precisely in comparing his parables with those which are most akin to them that the unexampled mastery with which Jesus handled this form of teaching is shown. The fact that in the rabbinic parables practically no use is made of nature and her doings is in itself remarkable; whereas the wealth and freedom of Jesus' method is most noticeable in the way in which he, a son of the people brought up far from the schools of the Scribes, steeped his parables in the world of nature. But the main difference is the same here as before. In the one case we have mere exposition of the Scriptures, in the other a living piety. There the parables are designed to illustrate the distorted ideas of a dead learning, and therefore often—though by no means always—themselves become distorted and artificial. Here the parable was handled by one whose whole soul was set, clearly and simply and with nothing to impede its vision, upon the real. Thus Jesus was and remains master of the parable. He *spoke*; the others stammered. In his parables Jesus becomes an artist; like the truest and greatest artists, he had the faculty of seeing things as they were, in all their wealth and variety; he discerned in them whatever had meaning and could serve as an example, and he had the gift of putting what he saw into simple and yet perfect shape. And so he created his work of art, the parable.

Jesus as Preacher and Healer

But all this he turned to the practical end of awakening and instructing the people. As he handled the parabolic form with artistic freedom and independence, so all other means towards this end lent themselves to his use. He could strike any note; he knew how to convince the brain by quiet persuasion and instruction, or how to bring heavenly consolation to those oppressed by the burden of existence; he could string his words to a steely energy when his object was to awaken moral heroism, or he could let them flash forth in passionate wrath when he had to annihilate an adversary. Not even humour did he lack;[1] satire and irony[2] he seldom made use of, but he was fond of expressing his meaning with paradoxical sharpness.[3] He always used the right word at the right place, and never mis-

---

[1] Matt. xi. 16 ff., Mark vii. 19; there is humour in the parable of the unjust steward, perhaps also in Luke xiv. 7 ff.

[2] In Matt. v. 22, his imitation of the language and tone of the Pharisees' petty casuistry is ironical; cf. Luke xi. 47.

[3] A better understanding of some of the sharpest and most daring sayings of Jesus is obtained when we grasp

took his means. And behind the perfected form of his discourse, there stood ever the mighty force of actuality which dominated the hearts of his hearers.

Side by side with his labour of teaching, the Gospels place his activity as a healer. "He taught and healed." It is significant of his ways and methods that he directed his attention and his efforts not to the spiritual alone. His heart was wrung by the physical needs of the people also, and in his eyes the physical and the spiritual were inextricably intermingled. He was in fact not so hyperspiritual as his admirers would often have him to be. On the other hand, he was no social reformer. In his own wandering life of scarcity and self-denial, he had found poverty to be no great evil; rather he regarded wealth as such. But wherever he came across real distress, he was ready to help; wherever he

the fact that they are consciously one-sided or paradoxical, *e.g.* Matt. v. 17, 29 f., 34, 39 f.; Mark vii. 15, 18 ff.; Luke xiv. 26; Mark x. 24 ff., and so forth.

Jesus as Preacher and Healer

met with illness and infirmity, he was ready to heal. Jesus may be regarded as exceptionally successful in his healing. The art of medicine was at that time in its earliest infancy, at any rate in the corner of the world where Jesus lived. No one had any conception of what was practicable or impracticable within its field. The physician pursued his craft with all manner of remedies, possible and impossible, good and bad, sometimes by proper means, more often with all the devices of quackery, faith-healing and magic, with utterings of the mysterious name of God, and even by the religious method of prayer. Jesus made use of religious and spiritual means alone. He spoke the healing word to the sick man, took him by the hand or laid his hand upon him; that was all. Only rarely does the tradition record his using any other means.[1] His method of healing may be called a psychical one; he stirred the forces of the inner life so powerfully that they reacted upon the outward bodily life. He healed the

---

[1] *E.g.* Mark vii. 32 ff.; viii. 22 ff.

sick by his immovable faith in his heavenly Father and the divine force working in him, and by awakening in the maimed and suffering the same faith in himself as the messenger of God. Thus his healing activity lies entirely within the bounds of what is psychologically conceivable, and this feature of the life of Jesus has nothing absolutely unique about it. The history of religion offers countless analogies to it down to the most recent times: we need only mention the cases of astonishing and undeniable healing which attended the pilgrimages to Lourdes, or the miracle- and prayer-healings of Blumhardt in Bad Boll. In these cases modern science speaks of the remarkable phenomena of suggestion, auto-suggestion,[1] and hypnotism; and in view of these analogies it will at any rate be well to draw the limits of the possible very widely with regard to our Gospel stories. We have to consider the peculiarly powerful impression which the person of Jesus was in a position to make, the almost

[1] Mark v. 25 is a clear case of auto-suggestion.

Jesus as Preacher and Healer

incalculable force of the people's confidence in this ever-successful doctor, and the childishness and naïveté of the population, which as yet made no speculations as to the limits of the possible and entertained no suspicion of the miraculous, and could therefore attain to the very verge of what was possible by the mere force of its confidence.

Nevertheless the limitations and the psychological conditions of Jesus' healing power may clearly be perceived even from the Gospel records. Where Jesus found no faith, he could effect no cures.[1] It is especially remarkable that among his miracles one particular class is brought forward again and again—the healing of demoniacs. Now in these demoniacs we recognise with perfect clearness the mentally unsound. We can even detect the individual forms of madness or of nervous derangement in the different stories: *e.g.* delirium in Mark v. 2 ff., catalepsy in Matt. xii. 22, epilepsy in Mark ix. 17 ff. The popular

[1] Mark vi. 5 ff.

imagination referred the mysterious and inexplicable phenomena pertaining to these diseases to the direct agency of evil spirits or demons, by whom the sick man was said to be possessed ; and Jesus, who was quite a son of his time with regard to these outward ideas, shared their belief. He cast out the demons by whom the sick were possessed. What actually made itself felt, however, through these naïve conceptions, held by Jesus and his patients alike, was the healing and soothing influence of his extraordinary force of soul, with the confidence of victory which it imparted. It was here, where the widest scope was given for the exercise of spiritual and personal influence, that Jesus' success in healing was evidently greatest. And even if he attained no permanent results with many of these poor sufferers, he yet succeeded very often in producing a temporary calm in their mental condition. Many of his healings were probably such cases of temporary cure, which were then followed by still more violent relapses. In such a case it was said that, though the demon had been driven out, he had returned with others worse than himself. Jesus' parable of the returning devil probably refers to such experiences as these, which had happened to him in the course of his healings.[1]

Jesus himself attached great value to his healing art. The casting out of demons was to him a clear sign of the immediate nearness of the Kingdom of God, which was to begin with the vanquishing of Satan and the evil spirits.[2] When the messengers sent by the Baptist asked him whether he were "He that cometh," he pointed in reply to his miraculous healings.[3] They were to him the proof of the actual presence of the blessed new age, in which all misery and want would disappear. He cried woe to the cities of Chorazin and Bethsaida,[4] because they had not believed in spite of all his signs and wonders. Yet he never regarded his miracles

---

[1] Matt. xii. 43–45. [2] Matt. xii. 28.
[3] Matt. xi. 2 ff. [4] Matt. xi. 20 ff.

as anything absolutely unique, or as in themselves sufficient to confirm him in the eyes of the multitude as the heaven-sent Messiah. He mentions it quite as a matter of course that the "sons of the Pharisees" cast out devils.[1] When the multitude asked him for a "sign," evidently, that is, for some quite abnormal miracle by which his Messiahship should be so fully established that not even the dullest apprehension could deny it longer, he indignantly refused their demand.[2] He himself looked upon his miracles as a sure sign for those who already believed—"If they hear not Moses and the prophets, neither will they be persuaded if one rise from the dead."[3] And when his disciples returned to him with joy, after they had succeeded in casting out demons, he told them that they should not rejoice that the demons were subject to them so much as that their names were written in heaven. In short, Jesus suppressed all enthusiasm on the

---

[1] Matt. xii. 27. [2] Mark viii. 11 f. ; Matt. xii. 38 f.
[3] Luke xvi. 31.

Jesus as Preacher and Healer

part of the miracle-hunters by his own strong inwardness and spiritual energy.

Then, as we know, our Gospel tradition transformed Jesus into a miracle-worker in the absolute and special sense. In the Gospels he has become the supernatural Son of God, who interferes directly, and through no psychological medium, with the course of physical life; raises the dead, walks upon the sea, commands the winds and the waves, and feeds thousands with a few loaves of bread; for whom in fact no limits to the possible exist. The devout community traced the simple outline of the human Jesus upon the gold background of the miraculous. Yet the outline is still relatively easy to detach from the background, for on a closer examination we may observe that the vast majority of the so-called miracle-stories of the life of Jesus lie actually within the limits of the psychologically conceivable, while with others the historical element lies immediately below the surface, and can be discovered by the removal of a few touches added by tradition. There are in fact but a very few stories which record an absolutely miraculous and impossible event, or one for which no analogy can be found. These few must then be cast aside as the mere outgrowths of legend. But in the miracle-stories which occupy so large a space in the Gospels, a distinctly historical kernel remains. They express one whole side of the life of Jesus, and an infinitely attractive one. Jesus grieved for the physical as well as the spiritual need of his people. He taught *and healed.* Let us look once more at the picture of Jesus as the successful physician, and consider how the simple folk must have welcomed this saviour in direst misery, and with what infinite trust they must have hung around him. Wherever he came, courage that had seemed hopeless revived, tired eyes grew bright, tired hands and arms were stretched out to him. Surely he was all-powerful, surely nothing would be impossible to him. All needs, both of body and soul, were brought to him for his healing touch. All day he was surrounded by the cry of pain and fear, by overwhelming trust and longing for help, by stammering prayers, rejoicings, tears of joy and of gratitude. And he healed all who came, so far as he was able, until exhaustion conquered him.

Meanwhile it must not be forgotten that Jesus lived and worked among his own people, and within the limits of Israel. The Gentiles did not at first come into consideration at all. He felt that he was sent to the lost sheep of the house of Israel,[1] and he directed his efforts upon the people as a whole. Nor did he mean to found in the band of disciples whom he gathered round him an order living apart from the people, a sect or a community. He meant to win the people of Israel to their God. With infinite patience he set to work upon the whole body of the people. "O Jerusalem, Jerusalem, how often would I have gathered thy children together!"[2] In

[1] Matt. xv. 24. [2] Matt. xxiii. 37.

the parable of the unfruitful fig-tree he symbolised his own faithful toil for the people in the figure of the vine-dresser.[1] He bore with the multitude untiringly, and could look down with kindly indulgence upon this mob of children who would not be guided by their Master, but considered that their heaven-sent leaders ought to be exactly what they themselves would have them be.[2] It is true that in the long run he could not blind himself to the impression that his labour with the masses was on the whole in vain. Not only the influential leaders of the people, the priests and Levites, the Scribes and the "rich men," had held themselves aloof from him and had now gone over to the party of open antagonism and bitter hostility. Even the masses, who had at first welcomed him with such boundless enthusiasm, he felt to be now slipping gradually from his hold. His judgments grow sharper and sharper upon the frivolous multitude, engrossed in the sensuous and the

[1] Luke xiii. 6–9.   [2] Matt. xi. 16 ff.

Jesus as Preacher and Healer 57

external, marching step by step to meet their ruin; gloomier and gloomier his prophecies of their future and their destiny.[1] Yet for all that he did not allow himself to be diverted from his task. He remained true to his people to the very end. Even in his last days he did not relax his attempts to stir the masses by his public actions. He made his entry into Jerusalem, and allowed himself to be acclaimed as Messiah. With his old impetuous energy he vehemently denounced the abuses in the Temple, and placed himself in the centre of public interest. He never even thought of transferring his activity to another sphere, and it was only reluctantly that he allowed a cure to be wrung from him in a Gentile country.[2] He forbade his disciples to enter the streets of the Gentiles or the cities of the Samaritans; never did he give a direct command to carry the Gospel to the Gentiles.[3]

[1] See below, pp. 90 f.   [2] Matt. xv. 21 f.
[3] Matt. x. 5. The command to " baptize all nations," in Matt. xxviii. 18 f., does not pretend to come from the " historical " Jesus even in the tradition. The prophecy

Indeed it is only on this assumption that we can explain the hesitating and unsympathetic attitude—to say the least—which the disciples afterwards maintained towards Paul's mission to the Gentiles.[1] Jesus never spoke more than dimly of a time in which the Gentiles also should enter the Kingdom of God.[2] Both in deed and in thought he remained true to his own people.

of Mark xiii. 10 is proved by the mere disturbance of the context to be a palpable interpolation; *cf.* the parallel in Luke xxi. 12 ff., where the words are absent.

[1] Gal. ii. 9, 11 ff.   [2] See below, Chap. V.

CHAPTER IV

Disciples and Opponents

THE result of these outward conditions necessarily was that, towards the end of his life, Jesus concentrated his personal efforts more and more upon his disciples. Here we have another most important feature of the life of Jesus: the fact that he gathered disciples round him. From among the total number of them an inner circle of followers was especially marked off, who came to be known later as the Twelve. Whether Jesus really chose twelve disciples at a particular moment in his life, as the Gospel tradition asserts, is an open question. Against such an assumption we have the fact that the Apostles' disciples show a certain divergence as to the names of these twelve.[1] Also, it may be doubted whether we ought to credit Jesus with so mechanical a proceeding as a selection determined by a sacred number. But the fact remains that a select band of disciples did gather round Jesus. The persons who composed it may partially have varied, and Jesus often appears to be attended by a still smaller circle, such as the faithful three, Peter, James, and John. It is possible that at the end of his life he was accidentally accompanied by exactly twelve adherents. And thus the Gospel tradition might have arisen.

Now what was Jesus' object in collecting his band of disciples? Not, at any rate, to found a community or church. The community of the followers of Jesus did not arise until after his death. There is, indeed, scarcely room for any other hypothesis than that Jesus wished to create out of his inner ring of disciples a picked body of missionaries, or

---

[1] See the lists of the apostles in Mark iii. 16-19; Matt. x. 2 f.; Luke vi. 14-16; Acts i. 13; and *cf.* John i. 43-49.

Disciples and Opponents   61

wandering preachers, through whom he hoped to give a wider circulation and a greater emphasis to his message of repentance and of the nearness of the Kingdom of God. Once, indeed, according to the Gospel record, Jesus did actually send his disciples forth, with the command to preach the coming of the Kingdom, and to teach and heal as he himself had done.[1] It is true that this report appears in the Gospels as a detached episode, without any connection with the rest of the narrative. It is a measure which on the one hand has no preparation or foundation, and on the other no consequences whatever. It makes a casual appearance, and vanishes equally swiftly; possibly it represents an attempt which, in face of the growing hopelessness of his position and his work, Jesus gave up as suddenly as he had undertaken it.

In any case, since the time of Paul, the Christian tradition has been unanimous on one point: that the inner band of disciples felt

[1] **Mark vi. 7 ff.**

themselves from the outset to be missionaries, and believed themselves to have been prepared and instructed by Jesus for that purpose. Hence it was that from these disciples Jesus demanded everything. To them he put the great alternative. He tore them away from family, wife, calling, home; he asked that they should forsake all, sell what they possessed, and give up parents, brethren, friends, and servants.[1] In them he sought to kindle the heroism that will dare all things, and the enthusiasm that burns for sacrifice. He taught them that no man might look back who had once set his hand to the plough.[2] They were to be the salt of the earth and the light of the world.[3] Courage to confess their faith even before the great and mighty, fear of God that knew no fear of man, hardness of heart towards their dear ones for God's sake, joy of battle that feared neither the sword nor even dissen-

---

[1] Mark i. 16 ff.; Luke xiv. 26, 33; Mark x. 21, 28 f.
[2] Luke ix. 62.
[3] Matt. v. 13 ff.; Luke xiv. 34, and *passim*.

sion among near and dear,—these were the virtues which he taught them.

But he gave them more than this, more than the equipment necessary for their future calling. " He appointed twelve, *that they might be with him*," says with direct simplicity the Evangelist Mark. Gradually the common life of wandering led by Jesus and his disciples grew from a means into an end. The missionary idea and training became less prominent, the moral companionship, with its intrinsic value, more and more so. Within the circle of his disciples, and in company with them, he created the first beginnings of a community-life. Jesus was with his disciples and they with him. We at this distance can but dimly augur what wealth, what freshness and earnestness filled this common life of Jesus and his disciples, for the records handed down by our Gospels are neither detailed nor intimate enough to admit of a clear vision. But here we may surely be permitted to exert the imagination. We behold Jesus, in the company of his closest friends, wandering in lonely places, sometimes on the mountains, where God seemed more visibly present to the soul, sometimes resting in remote hamlets, now in the solitude of the desert, now in a boat upon the sea. In this way a life was led free from all restraint of circumstance or of petty affairs, far from the noise of the world, on the heights and in the silence, wholly absorbed in the personal and the spiritual. The first steps towards a new life of brotherhood were taken here, in stillness and privacy; it was the first wonderful stirring of a new humanity. We in our time, however, can but stand reverently afar off, before the veil which hides these beginnings from our sight.

Around this narrow circle there gathered then a further band of followers and friends, and of spectators interested or excited in many different shades and degrees. Not of all his disciples did Jesus make such austere and harsh demands as of those whom he had chosen to be missionaries. He had friends in the villages

Disciples and Opponents 65

and homesteads, under the conditions of ordinary life, among houses and families in many directions. For it was precisely among the common folk that he loved to find his followers. They were the "little ones" of whom he often speaks, the uneducated and the humble to whom God had revealed what He had hidden from the "wise."[1] Woe unto him who should give cause of stumbling to one of these simple children, who were incapable of help or counsel of their own.[2] Above all, however (and we shall have occasion to speak more fully of this fundamental characteristic later on), he felt himself drawn to those whom good society had placed under the ban; to those who had refused in any way to fall in with the forms of the ruling Pharisaic piety, and were therefore decried as sinners and worldlings; to the class of tax-gatherers, boycotted by Jewish popular fanaticism as the tools of the foreigner's rule, and lower still to the wholly outcast and lost, the

[1] Matt. xi. 25.   [2] Luke xvii. 2; Matt. xviii. 14.

fallen women and the prostitutes.¹ Yet gentlefolk came to him too, for now and then a rich man of the upper classes would make his appearance; respectable women followed in his train;² occasionally a scribe³ or a distinguished and influential councillor⁴ would show themselves among those half won. Scribes and Pharisees came to dispute with him; aristocratic Sadducees came to have a sight of the holy man of whom such wonders were told; even King Herod grew uneasy.⁵ Thus all the many-coloured life of the people thronged round the figure of Jesus.

The picture would not be complete if we did not briefly touch upon his adversaries. On the whole, it may be said that all who possessed influence or consideration with the people ultimately found themselves on the side of his avowed opponents. Yet it is remarkable that the kernel of the opposition

---

[1] John vii. 53–viii. 11; Luke vii. 36–50, viii. 2.
[2] Luke viii. 3.   [3] Mark xii. 28.
[4] Mark xv. 43.   [5] Mark vi. 14–16.

Disciples and Opponents 67

was not formed by the priests and religious functionaries of Israel. The priestly aristocracy of Jerusalem, which ruled the councils of the country, did indeed finally bring about his fall. But Jesus only came into close contact with it at the end of his life, and we do not know with any certainty how the sudden hostility of this class arose. The adversaries with whom he had to contend in Galilee were other than these: they were the Scribes and Pharisees.

The bitterest enemies of Jesus, and the true antipodes to all that he stood for, were the *Scribes*. However closely he resembled them in the outward forms of his activity, in the spirit of it he and they were at opposite poles. On the one hand was the artificiality of a hair-splitting and barren erudition, on the other the fresh directness of the layman and the son of the people; here was the product of long generations of misrepresentation and distortion, there was simplicity, plainness, and freedom; here a clinging to the petty and the insignificant, a burrowing in the dust, there a constant dwelling upon the essential and a great inward sense of reality; here the refinement of casuistry, formula- and phrase-mongering, there the straightforwardness, severity, and pitilessness of the preacher of repentance; here a language which was scarcely to be understood, there the inborn power of the mighty orator; here the letter of the law and there the living God. It was like the meeting of water and fire. This close corporation of the professionally learned could never forgive the simple outsider for making a greater effect than they, and for the fact that the people listened to him. Between these two there must have been mortal enmity from the outset. And on the other hand, Jesus' love of truth and feeling for reality, offended by such caricatures of true piety,[1] broke through all the limits of forbearance, self-restraint, and con-

---

[1] It is to be assumed that from the average here considered an exception must be made in favour of a few celebrated and really pious rabbis, such as Hillel, Gamaliel, and some others.

sideration, and allowed the passionate wrath of his soul to pour forth far and wide. In contrast to them, his life and personality gains that touch of relentlessness and pugnacity which could ill be spared in it.

His attitude towards the Pharisees was the same as his attitude towards the Scribes. The Pharisees were no more than the outposts of the Scribes among the laity—the pietists of Jewish orthodoxy, the devout after the spirit and the pattern of rabbinism. But whereas in Judæa the spirit of rabbinic devoutness had almost completely triumphed, and Jewish piety had become practically Pharisaic, in Galilee the Pharisees seem only to have formed small centres at the time of Jesus' appearance. Even later, Galilee was regarded by the Scribes as an unfruitful land almost lost to the cause of piety, and its people as vulgar, stupid, and unhearing. Still, Pharisaic circles were to be found there, and naturally considered themselves to have a monopoly of righteousness. Here in Galilee Jesus could enter the lists amid the delight of the simple-hearted believers and the rejoicing and applause of the multitude. He did not fail to do so. "Except your righteousness exceed the righteousness of the Scribes and Pharisees, ye shall in nowise enter into the kingdom of heaven."[1]

But this antagonism of Jesus to the Scribes and Pharisees has taken us from the outward forms of his activity to its material content, and it is impossible to realise him without to some extent examining the latter.

[1] Matt. v. 20.

BOOK II

THE TEACHING OF JESUS

CHAPTER V

The Kingdom of God

JESUS took up his ministry with the cry that the Kingdom of God was at hand,[1] and the idea that the Kingdom was approaching is throughout the dominant note of his teaching. The Kingdom of God—there was no need for Jesus to enter into detailed explanations of what he meant by the phrase, for every child in the country could have told him. At the moment that Jesus took up his preaching, the people in whose midst he appeared lay trampled into complete subjection. Harsh masters ruled the land; in Judæa the accursed Romans, in Galilee a

[1] Matt. iv. 17.

prince set up by them, who came of the detested house of Herod; harsh tax-collectors, creatures of the despotic overlords, plundered the people, and the people themselves, simple, hard-working and deprived of all the pleasures of life, felt themselves lost in a world that had become vast, hostile, and cold. Their spiritual leaders told them that they were not pious enough, and set them in the thorny path of the law, only to blame them if they followed it unwillingly and found themselves wholly unable to obey the multifarious rules of the "true" piety which the Scribes had devised in their learned ease. But deep in their hearts lay the hope of the Kingdom of God, of those great and marvellous things which Israel should still live to see, according to its ancient prophecies; of the grand procession of events, the reversal of all existing circumstance, the dawn of the new golden day, which was to leap up at last with its broad beams of light and scatter the shadows of poverty and want, hunger and thirst, and God-forsaken longing.

The Kingdom of God

Then came Jesus, preaching "Rejoice and be glad: blessed are ye, for the kingdom of God is at hand!" How different was his message from that of the Baptist! John had appeared in the south, where he saw around him only the insolence of a barren piety of erudition, the pride of a degenerate priestly caste, and the licentious frivolity of a city population. Hence his preaching of the Kingdom had become fierce and hard, and entirely concentrated upon the ideas of judgment, terror, and destruction. We shall see below that even with Jesus the words, "The kingdom of God is at hand," had their reverse sense of "The Judgment cometh"; but at first he preferred to strike the other fundamental note of the message of the Kingdom. The tidings he brought were tidings of promise; he saw that the first necessity was to let a bright ray of hope and joy into the dull and weary souls of this anxious people, and so he cried, "Blessed are ye poor, for yours is the kingdom of heaven." When in after years the disciples of Jesus tried to express his work and his whole being in a single word, they called the story of his life the εὐαγγέλιον, or good tidings.

The substance of these tidings was: "The kingdom (or *reign*)[1] of God is at hand." Jesus did not say to the people, "The moment is come: now see ye that the Kingdom of God appear: compel its coming," for that was the misleading cry of the fanatical patriots who had already begun to show themselves, especially in Galilee. Rather his immovable belief was that the ordinary doings and earthly labour of men could not bring the Kingdom of God one finger's-breadth nearer to mankind. In his view the coming of the Kingdom lay wholly in the sphere of the future and the supernatural. The living, all-powerful God, and He alone, would set up His marvellous reign. But He would indeed set it up, and

---

[1] The Greek word Basileia signifies both "kingdom" and "reign," and bears now the one and now the other of these two closely connected meanings.

that soon. Therefore lift up your heads and await the miraculous to-come.

How strange and naïve do these ideas of Jesus seem to us at the first glance! How closely does his preaching appear to be interwoven in this respect with the thoughts and hopes of contemporary Judaism! How easy do we find it to calculate that he, together with his countrymen and his disciples, was mistaken in his expectation of the immediate nearness of this mighty supernatural change![1]

Hence it is that many attempts have been made to give the preaching of Jesus a more modern dress, and to read into his words all manner of "deeper" and "more original" ideas. It has above all been insisted that in the words of Jesus the Kingdom of God

---

[1] It is impossible to deny this expectation of an immediate end on the part of Jesus. It is proved not only by certain clear and distinct sayings (such as Mark ix. 1, xiii. 30, Matt. x. 23), but principally by the whole tone of his preaching of the future, in which he concentrates the attention of his disciples upon the end as though it were an immediately impending event.

frequently appears to mean an *already present* and *inward* power. It is indeed admitted that, strictly speaking, the idea of the Kingdom in Jesus' preaching is an eschatological one, *i.e.* that the Kingdom of God is represented entirely as a future and yet-to-be-hoped-for state, and above all as a supernatural event which would be brought about by the miraculous power of God, in close connection with a marvellous outward metamorphosis of all existing circumstance. Side by side with this, however, it is contended that in his preaching of the Kingdom Jesus expresses the idea that this same Kingdom of God was already present, growing and ripening inwardly and by inward transformation of existing circumstance; that it was to be built up by the moral actions of mankind, beginning with those of Jesus and his disciples, and even that it represented the community of those who were morally and spiritually bound together by such actions. These modern ideas, however, must be entirely rejected in so far as they concern Jesus' conception of the Kingdom of God. Such an interpretation introduces without cogent reason a scarcely conceivable confusion and inconsistency into the clear and simple mental world of Jesus.

Certain sayings of Jesus are indeed cited in support of this view. Thus the incident is adduced in which he cries out against the sneers of the Pharisees: "If I by the Spirit of God cast out devils, then is the kingdom of God come upon you."[1] Here it is certainly true that in his eyes the Kingdom of God was already present. But it must not be forgotten that this is a saying spoken at a moment of great excitement, in which he likens his own miracles and casting out of devils directly to the miraculous power of God, with which He would presently set up His Kingdom and trample Satan, the prince of all the devils, underfoot. The Kingdom of God—and here lies the essential point—remains within the sphere of the marvellous

[1] Matt. xii. 28.

and the supernatural. The idea of an inward development by preaching and social labour is not even remotely present. The same thought is expressed in Jesus' answer to the Pharisees, when they had boasted that they could calculate the hour of the coming of the Kingdom by methods of human ingenuity: "The kingdom of God cometh not with observation: neither shall they say, Lo here! or there! for lo, the kingdom of God is in the midst of you."[1] It had escaped the inquiring Pharisees that the beginnings of the Kingdom were already manifesting themselves in their presence. Here again we have an inspired and paradoxical saying of Jesus in which he was certainly thinking of his own actions, but in their miraculous, not in their moral aspect; as on another occasion, when the envoys of the Baptist asked him whether he were "He that cometh," *i.e.* whether the Kingdom were to be

[1] Luke xvii. 20. Perhaps too the right translation is, "For lo, the Kingdom of God will (suddenly) be among you." In that case the whole passage would refer to the future Kingdom of God.

The Kingdom of God 79

expected with him, he pointed for answer to the wonders he had wrought.[1]

But the principal support for the view here disputed is sought in the so-called Parables of the Kingdom; though scarcely with justice. When Jesus in the parable of the grain of mustard-seed[2] speaks of the rapid and enormous growth of the Kingdom of Heaven, we must remember that the mustard-shrub was a garden plant which sprang up in a single summer. Thus there is no question in this parable of the development of centuries, in which the Kingdom of God should gradually rise victorious over the nations, but of an inconceivably swift and dazzling coming of the golden age, now appearing in its first tentative beginnings through the activity of Jesus in miracle-working and casting out of demons. Here too, therefore, we have the marvellously rapid approach of the Kingdom *in the miraculous*, and are very far removed from

---

[1] Matt. xi. 2 ff.
[2] Mark iv. 30 ff.; Luke xiii. 18-21; Matt. xiii. 31 f.

the modern idea of slow development. Again, in the other well-known parable where the Kingdom of God is compared to a pearl for which the merchant who finds it gives all that he has to buy it,[1] this does not mean that the Kingdom of God was a present possession, but precisely the contrary. The parable is meant to show the necessity of hazarding all present goods for the sake of a future and yet-to-be-acquired good. Even in the parable of the peasant who casts seed upon the earth, and can then do nothing but await the harvest, the emphasis lies not upon the description of the gradual growth of the seed, but on the idea that the corn ripens to the harvest "of itself." The Kingdom of God will not come by man's assistance, but of itself, or rather from above, from the God who gives the harvest. Man is to do his duty, but when that is done he must wait until God utters His *fiat*.

Thus the fact remains that the Kingdom of

[1] Matt. xiii. 45.

The Kingdom of God

God as Jesus preached it lay principally in the domain of the future, and wholly in the domain of the miraculous.[1] It was God's Kingdom pure and simple, to be established by the omnipotent God at the moment when He upheaved the heavens and the earth, raised the dead, and vanquished and destroyed the devil and all his angels. It was for this kingdom that Jesus taught his disciples to pray so fervently "Thy kingdom come." And if now and again he seemed to see some portion of it already present in his own works, this was only during the rush of enthusiasm that seized him when he had reached some pinnacle of success. The course of his own life and work was to

[1] The best known of the so-called Parables of the Kingdom, that of the sower, is not, strictly speaking, a Parable of the Kingdom at all. Jesus is there dealing with the effect or non-effect of his own preaching. In the saying of Matt. xi. 11, that he that is but little in the Kingdom of Heaven is greater than John the Baptist, the word Kingdom of Heaven is certainly almost equivalent to "society of the disciples of Jesus." But this saying, which alone does not fit in with the general sense of Jesus' preaching of the Kingdom, probably belongs to the language of the later community.

show him that the road to the Kingdom of God was not so straight after all, but reached its end at last through suffering and death.

Nor is the very widespread idea that the eschatological hopes of his countrymen were altogether spiritualised by Jesus to be accepted as it stands. When he told the Sadducees that in that blessed future life there would be neither marrying nor giving in marriage,[1] he was certainly spiritualising the vulgar notion, but in all probability he was not expressing anything entirely new, for this must have been the conviction of a great many truly religious men at the time he uttered it. On the other hand, when Jesus spoke of the future, he was not thinking of a colourless and purely heavenly beyond, but pictured it to himself as a state of things existing upon this earth—though of course a transfigured earth—and in his own land. In the Gospel of Matthew we certainly find the expression "Kingdom of Heaven" again and

[1] Mark xii. 25.

The Kingdom of God

again upon his lips, but we must not be misled by it. For we know that even if Jesus did make use of the term "Kingdom of Heaven," he meant neither more nor less by it than if he had said "Kingdom of God." He would, in fact, merely have been following the usage of his time and surroundings, by which it was customary to avoid mentioning the name of God, and instead of "the fear of God" or "the hand of God," to say "the fear of Heaven" and "the hand of Heaven." From the expression "Kingdom of Heaven," therefore, it is impossible to draw any inference as to the place and nature of the kingdom proclaimed by Jesus. Nor was Jesus at all afraid of painting the joys of the glorious future to his disciples in rich and sensuous colours. He speaks of the filling of the hungry,[1] of eating and drinking and sitting at table with the patriarchs in the Kingdom of Heaven;[2] he is fond of describing the delights of the future under the simile of a feast or a wedding, and

[1] Luke vi. 21.   [2] Matt. viii. 11.

he prophesies a time when he and his would drink of the fruit of the vine in the Kingdom of Heaven.[1] It shows a want of understanding of the popular simplicity of Jesus' preaching to see in all this merely parable and symbolic expression. However hard it may seem, it is our duty to accustom ourselves to the idea that in his preaching Jesus was very largely a child of his age and a faithful son of his country.

Nevertheless we have so far considered but one aspect of the preaching of Jesus concerning the Kingdom of God. If nothing more were to be said about it, it would merely have been an unheard-of accident that the labour and preaching of Jesus should still have contained the germs of a world-religion and of a universal transformation and renewal such as we mortals have never beheld elsewhere. Though steeped in the eschatological hopes of his time and country, he yet succeeded in altering and purifying them at the critical

[1] Luke xxii. 18 (and *cf.* xxii. 16).

point, and in breaking through the limits which hemmed them in. For at the time of Jesus the eschatological hopes of the Jews, wherever they were truly alive, were tied and bound to their spirit of nationalism. They were the hopes of the people of Israel. Their central idea was that Israel should one day come to its own and wield the sovereignty which belonged to it of right. The Kingdom of God was neither more nor less than the rule of Israel. That the hated tribe of Rome should one day lie grovelling in the dust with Israel's foot upon its neck, that the Messiah, God's chosen King, should rule the world from Jerusalem with might and glory, that the nations should come and pay tribute before Israel, and that Jerusalem and its temple should be built up again in splendour, while the saints bore rule throughout the land of Palestine—such were the hopes which occupied the first place in the pious Israelite's outlook, whenever he gazed into the future. Even if they were sometimes mingled with more profound ideas of the nearness of God or the forgiveness of sins, of purity of heart or the outpouring of the Spirit, these were and remained the cardinal points. If in the poems of some of the Jewish seers idealism did spread its wings more freely, its flight was clogged by the leaden weight of the national hopes, now grown into fanaticism, which impeded all free movement. In short, the eschatological hopes of the Jews remained fettered to the nation, and therefore to the earth.

But in the soul of Jesus a wonderful deliverance was wrought. It worked its way wholly from within outwards. Naturally, indeed, when he spoke of the Kingdom of God, he thought first and foremost of a kingdom in Israel, and he would also have taken it for granted that the empire of Rome could not subsist side by side with the empire of God. His gaze was directed upon Israel; he bound himself to its people by his works, and felt himself sent to the lost sheep of the house of Israel; he even described the future as a sitting at meat in company with the patriarchs of the old covenant. All this is true; yet on the other hand it formed but the mould into which his genius poured a new content. Here at last we grasp the secret of that marvellous power by which dross was transformed into the clearest, finest gold. His inmost religious character stands revealed: the sense that *God* was infinitely greater and infinitely more than all the world besides—a reality beside which all other realities paled and sank. Only for this reality had Jesus thought and feeling, and hence he proclaimed the Kingdom *of God*. That Israel should rule and the Romans be laid low was nothing to him, or at most it was but the outward form in which God's purpose would be fulfilled; the earthly side of the promise of the Kingdom did not interest him; it left him cold. What did fill his soul to the brim was the thought that God would come, that God would bear rule, that righteousness would conquer and good triumph. Whereas in

Jewish literature the expression "Kingdom of God" is but seldom met with, Jesus made it the very foundation of his preaching. The Jewish patriots looked for much else besides the Kingdom and the rule of God—above all for their own kingdom, the "kingdom of the saints"; Jesus spoke only of the Kingdom of God. And thus, without saying it directly, he purified the hopes of the Jewish people in marvellous wise and freed them from their limitations. When he speaks of the blessed and glorious future, all notes of confused passion and worldly hatred die away; he calls it the time when the pure in heart shall see God, when the peacemakers shall be called the sons of God, when the merciful shall obtain mercy, when the good and faithful servants of God shall win their reward, when the multiplied talents shall be shown and the new tasks assigned, when evil will disappear and good rise triumphant. It is astonishing to see how utterly he rejects all the national and political hopes of the Jews, that vital element of their eschatological faith. If occasionally some note of it is to be met with, if Jesus actually spoke of a time in which his disciples should sit upon twelve thrones judging the twelve tribes of Israel,[1] these are but the last faint echoes of an old melody, sounding on into the new song.

It is this, too, that explains the certainty and confidence with which Jesus proclaimed the Kingdom of God, and continued to do so in spite of all the disappointments of his career. At first, and even far on into his ministry, he combined the idea of the Kingdom of God with that of his own people of Israel. To the very end he spent his labours upon them alone. And yet, unless all our tradition is at fault—and we are obliged to trust to it if we do not wish to assert that Jesus had a less keen perception of the nature of things than the prophets of old—Jesus must have recognised more and more clearly as his ministry went on that his own people,

[1] Matt. xix. 28.

amongst whom he worked, did not answer to his expectations.¹ As his predecessor John the Baptist had seen the judgment hanging over this people, so Jesus saw, to his horror, the children of the Kingdom cast forth into the outer darkness.² Israel was to him as the unfruitful fig-tree, which deserved to wither because it produced leaves without blossoms.³ In the fate of those who were killed by the falling of the tower of Siloam, or of the Galileans whom Pilate had murdered in the Temple, he saw, as in a mirror, the fate of the whole nation.⁴ He prophesied that, as in the days of Noah and Lot, so should the judgment fall upon this frivolous multitude;⁵ he saw his countrymen hastening along the broad road to destruction,⁶ and we must surely assume, with the

[1] For what follows *cf.* p. 56, above.
[2] Matt. viii. 12.
[3] Mark xi. 12–14 (20). The Gospel tradition has here turned a parable or a symbolic action (the cursing of the fig-tree) into an extravagant miracle.
[4] Luke xiii. 1 ff., 4 ff.
[5] Luke xvii. 26 ff.   [6] Luke xiii. 24 ff.

The Kingdom of God

tradition, that he foretold how the Temple, the very centre of contemporary Judaism, should have not one stone left upon another.[1] Yet in spite of all this, the confidence and joyousness of his preaching of the Kingdom remained unshaken. To him God was greater than the world and of more account than his own countrymen, and the rule of God was something other than and independent of the rule of Israel. He had already promised his disciples, in a time of anxiety and distress, that they should proclaim upon the house-tops what he had told them in their ear.[2] It is true that in his short life he never accomplished the outward breach with Israel. He began by bidding his disciples go into no street of the Gentiles and into no city of the Samaritans,[3] and told them that they would not have carried the Gospel to all the cities of Israel " till the Son of Man be come."[4] He refused to help the foreign woman because

---

[1] Mark xiii. 1 f. [2] Matt. x. 26 f.
[3] Matt. x. 5. [4] Matt. x. 23.

he was "not sent except unto the lost sheep of the house of Israel." And yet in an intuitive, prophetic way he was able to conceive and to face the idea of the separateness of the Kingdom of God from the people of Israel. Here the Old Testament came to his aid. It told him of the men of Nineveh who accepted Jonah's preaching of repentance, of the queen of the south who came to hear Solomon,[1] of Elijah and the widow of Zarephath, of Elisha and Naaman the Syrian;[2] and many another prophetic utterance about the blindness of the chosen people and the coming of the nations to God must have sunk into his heart. Experiences of his own were not lacking, such as the incidents of the centurion at Capernaum and of the Canaanitish woman who importuned him to help her. Then there flashed into his soul the thought that the sons of the Kingdom should be cast forth into the outer darkness, while many should come from the east and the west and

[1] Matt. xii. 40 ff.   [2] Luke iv. 24 ff.

The Kingdom of God

sit down with Abraham and Isaac and Jacob in the Kingdom of Heaven.[1] And further, when he declared that the vineyard should be taken away from the present husbandmen and given to others, or that the guests who were bidden to the marriage feast should not taste of it, but should give place to others gathered together from the highways and hedges, he was contemplating here too, in a suggestive and prophetic way, the same tremendous transformation.[2]

Even if one were inclined to refer these and other indications to a later Christian tradition, two things remain untouched. The first is that the triumphant conviction that the King-

[1] Matt. viii. 11.

[2] Luke xiv. 16 ff.; Matt. xxii. 2–10; Mark xii. 1 ff. In these two parables it is of course open to question whether Jesus meant to contrast the leaders of the people with the simple lower classes, or the nation itself with the Gentiles. When Luke mentions a twofold invitation after the refusal of the originally invited guests, he was probably thinking first of the poorer classes of the people, and after them of the Gentiles; so that he must have understood the original parable, which contained but one invitation (*cf.* Matt.), in the former sense.

dom of God must come, which afterwards filled the disciples of Jesus from the very beginning, the conviction that whatever attitude men might take up towards it, the rule of God must find its way into their hearts; the joyous, fearless, and undaunted mission-work of the little flock, upon which Paul was able to proceed in spite of the nationalist limitations it had at first suffered under: these things are spirit of Jesus' spirit, and flame of the fire of his soul.

Still more important, however, is the consideration that even if Jesus did not himself draw the external consequences of his own preaching of the Kingdom, if all these bold words were merely the later voice of his community, we should still have in them the logical consummation of Jesus' preaching of the Kingdom of God. For in that preaching the decisive severance from the national element had already occurred; with the idea of the Kingdom of God the universalism of the Gospel is already present in embryo. By

The Kingdom of God

lifting the idea of the Kingdom into the religious sphere—a sphere in which earthly hopes and national passions must necessarily sink, with everything unclean, before the majesty of the omnipresent God—Jesus freed religion at the critical point from the nation, so far at least as the nation constituted a danger and a limitation to religion. All that followed upon this was merely the external working out. Even when the bonds of nationality were finally and visibly broken, when Paul carried the torch of the Gospel over to the Gentiles, Jesus' preaching of the Kingdom of God did not lose its freshness. Better even than the inmost core of Paul's preaching, Jesus' announcement of the approaching rule of God was grasped and understood. It won its way in its original purity, freedom, and earnestness; what was temporal in it was freely cast aside, while the eternal elements were easily absorbed: "The kingdom of God cometh, God himself cometh. Blessed are the pure in heart, for they shall see God."

But the objection may be raised that, even if Jesus' preaching of the Kingdom was of decisive importance for the first centuries of Christian development, for us it has no longer any significance. And it is certainly true that in its naïve form it seems very far removed from all modern experience. History, the irrevocable march of events, have proved that the expectation of an immediate and mighty transformation was mistaken. So much is beyond dispute. For us the idea of the possibility of any universal change has retreated at least to the extreme limit of our thought; and indeed, in the shape in which Jesus announced it, it has become absolutely inconceivable. Through the influence which the Copernican system has exercised upon our minds, our idea of the physical world has become other than that upon which the eschatological hopes of Jesus rested, in their form at any rate.

Nevertheless even here it will be advisable not to throw away hastily and rashly things of permanent value and importance in the preaching of Jesus. The form of his preaching of the Kingdom was transitory, and its husk has already shed itself. But within the form there lies an eternal content. The Gospels lay it down with energy and decision that this world, with its events and its labours, is not an endless affair, continually repeating itself and revolving in a circle, but that everything has its ending, its aim and goal, which rest in the hand of God and lie determined beforehand in His mind. And all that appears to us strange, fantastic, and childish in Jesus' preaching of the Kingdom we must regard as the necessary body without which the spirit hidden within it could not come to life—as the transient and glittering raiment cast over eternal ideas. Those to whom this notion of a final and conclusive world's end seems too remote, should consider that our own little life, ringed round by birth and death, suddenly appearing out of the darkness of night, out of an unknown Whence, will die away again all too soon and pass out into an unknown Whither, of which we, as disciples of Jesus, can only dimly believe and hope that it will be an existence nearer to God. If Jesus expected the irruption and appearance of this unknown world in the immediate future, we can no longer share his expectation; yet our own end, our own entry into the darkness of the Beyond, still remains a thing of the immediate future. And with this in mind we can still pray in the spirit of Jesus, though not in the direct and literal sense of his words, "Thy kingdom come." And for us too, his saying shines with everlasting light, "Blessed are the pure in heart, for they shall see God."

CHAPTER VI

Jesus' Conception of God

How near and tangible the Gospel of Jesus is to us in its main ideas and fundamental features will best be seen when we penetrate still deeper, past the outward form, with its temporal limitations, to the spirit beyond. Here then, as in all other religions, we find it to be the simple faith in God. The form of Jesus' preaching, conditioned as it was by his time and surroundings, was, "The kingdom of God is at hand: God cometh." But we shall reach its spirit when we ask: "Who was the God of Jesus, whose coming he announced? What did the word *God* mean to him?"

One thing becomes clear at once, in looking

at the general picture of Jesus' life and personality: that for him God was a reality, clear, living, and present above all others. For the devout Jewish patriots of his time and surroundings God was certainly a reality too, but another equally strong and closely connected reality was the people of Israel, with its claim on happiness and universal dominion. For them the rule of God meant the rule of Israel. And since Israel now lay trampled underfoot, they could never enjoy or feel sure of the corresponding reality of God. Their faith and confidence became mingled with torturing doubts; the religious community grew uneasy, exasperated, and subject to all sorts of fluctuating moods, which were ever ready to pass into their opposites. High-spirited confidence alternated in rapid succession with gnawing uncertainty; boastful exaltation of one's own merit with abject humility, pride with grovelling penitence. But, above all, faith in a living and ever-present God who interfered with a strong hand in the history

Jesus' Conception of God 101

of the present, was entirely lost sight of. They could neither conceive nor feel such a presence, for their eyes were fixed upon this broken and low-fallen people. Hence they directed all the fervour of their faith towards the future; they believed in a God who, though far distant now, would in the future draw near again. Their faith became in fact a mere matter of hope. On the other hand, those who held themselves more aloof from the popular piety and the exaggerated national hopes, the specifically pious, the learned class who were wholly absorbed in the law and the Scriptures, were apt to let reality and the feeling for it vanish from their grasp. They created a fictitious reality for themselves in their rabbinic schools, in the silence of their own chambers, beside their rolls of the law; and in the place of the living presence of God—though indeed this was not wholly lost to view—they set the spider's webs of their own learning, in which they claimed to have caught the absolute will of God. What they cared for was the ingenuity and erudition necessary for the interpretation of Scripture; they delighted in disputation for its own sake and in distorted subtleties, and enjoyed the esteem and veneration of numerous pupils whose ambition was to become even as their masters were before them.

But to Jesus God was once more a reality. That, as we have seen, was the secret of his preaching of the Kingdom. And because God was to him a fact which far surpassed all others in importance, even his belief in his own people, he was in a position to lift the idea of the Kingdom of God into a higher sphere.

Moreover, God was to him a *present* reality, not merely a matter of hope and of the future. At first sight it might seem, after what has been said above, that this was not the case, for Jesus proclaims first and foremost the *approaching* God and the approaching Kingdom. Yet future and present are in reality marvellously blended into one. For while

Jesus' Conception of God 103

in the main the Jewish patriots expected from the future and the action of God something of which they were now experiencing the direct contrary—namely, the revival and universal supremacy of their own people—Jesus in the main expected from the future nothing essentially different from what he was already experiencing in his own breast—namely, the sense of nearness to God, the vision of God, the satisfying of the great longing and hunger after God, the triumphant victory of good over evil. The coming God was already there before his soul in tangible presence, and the future was to him so sure and certain because his God was a present reality.

And a most living reality too. Never was God felt as such a living presence in the life of any man. Jesus breathed in an atmosphere of God; everything in his life, so far as we know it, was religion. With every word he directed his own and his hearers' souls towards God; in every situation of his life, even the most difficult, he took refuge with

God and listened to His voice; all joy became a thanksgiving, and all pain a submission to God's will. Everything in him is aimed at the highest and ultimate goal; nowhere is there any slackening or trifling or pursuit of side-issues. Piety informs his life like a never-failing electric current, flowing with quiet and even force through his soul, free from all hindrance and distraction. At certain points indeed a stronger tension may be observed, and the sparks leap up with destroying energy, especially when he meets with opposition. Well may we guess, too, that in the depths of that soul many a battle had been fought through of which the children of ordinary life have no conception; but in all that he shows of his inner life the strongest impressions are those of harmonious calm and firm, concentrated power. He himself was conscious of the greatest antithesis to his own being when he came across some purely worldly life, given up to the present with its unrest, its cares, divisions, and confusions. He scourged it in many a vigorous parable:[1] "Thou foolish one, this night is thy soul required of thee; and the things which thou hast prepared, whose shall they be?" To his disciples he taught above all things the great *sursum corda*, the wealth of the heart in God; he sought to lift them into his own sphere, to which the cares and calculations of the world, and the noise and trouble of every day, were unable to penetrate.[2]

Further, we must observe that for Jesus God was a purely spiritual, personal reality. "God is a spirit, and they that worship Him must worship in spirit and truth,"[3]—so did one of his greatest disciples sum up Jesus' message and desires on this point. His whole intercourse with God lies in the realm of the spiritual and personal. Nowhere is any value attached to outward means and forms. The entire sacred cult of his country contributed nothing to the true core of his piety. If

---

[1] Luke xii. 15 ff.; xvi. 9 ff.   [2] Matt. vi. 19 ff.
[3] John iv. 24.

he did once exert himself in grim earnest for the holiness and purity of the Temple service, perhaps this was only because of his general dislike of all pseudo-holiness and hypocrisy. Nor should we forget that Jesus' whole life and work, apart from their ending, were enacted on a stage far removed from the Temple and its cult. Jesus could say, in the manner of the old prophets, "I desire mercy, and not sacrifice";[1] he set reconciliation with one's brother[2] and fulfilment of one's filial duty[3] unhesitatingly before the service of the altar. He could endure the thought that not one stone of the Temple should be left upon another,[4] and the bold words "Destroy this temple that is made with hands, and in three days I will build another made without hands," played an important part in the charges brought against him.[5] It is true that with this inward detachment of religion from the official cult, Jesus was only completing a

---

[1] Matt. ix. 13. [2] Matt. v. 23 f. [3] Mark vii. 10 ff.
[4] Mark xiii. 1 f. [5] Mark xiv. 58.

movement which had already been stirring for a considerable time within the Jewish body. The Temple cult had long ceased to play the part which had belonged to it in the first centuries of the renovated Temple. Though outwardly still an object of splendour, it had lost its inward significance for and power over the souls of the pious nation. The law had stepped in beside the cult, rabbinism beside the degenerate and worldly priesthood, the synagogue beside the Temple, prayer and alms-giving beside sacrifice. But Jesus not only completed what was already begun, he also delivered the true, spiritual piety from the dangerous enemies which had sprung up in the place of the old cult—from the corruption of religion by legalism and casuistry, from the glorification of the letter and the blind clinging to use and wont.

He effected this deliverance by inward means, not by any outward agitation and violence. Circumcision, tithes, the keeping of the Sabbath, prayer and alms-giving—all these he left standing as they were, so long as they were not actively harmful. But he left them in the position which belonged to them, namely, on the outskirts and in the forecourt of the religious life. He taught that they were matters of indifference, and that they might be done while the "weightier matters" were not left undone.[1] Only where the external enveloped and choked the spiritual, did he ruthlessly destroy it. The path along which he took his followers led upwards to the pure heights of the spirit. He set them face to face, not with use and wont, the claims and the letter of the law, and its painful and exact fulfilment, but with the living God. And while with sure though gentle hand he released religion from its ancient forms, he nevertheless created *no new forms*, nothing material to place between God and His disciples. Yet how soon was this altered by the community he left behind him! How soon did they return to the view that, even though

[1] Matt. xxiii. 23.

Jesus' Conception of God

faith and the personal relation of the believer to God was the main point, yet material, mystical transactions and external ceremonies could not be dispensed with! Baptism became to the Christians an actual immersion with an external, miraculous, cleansing, and hallowing effect, brought about by the agency of consecrated water; and the solemn bestowal of the name at baptism was intended as a protection against the evil spirits working in the world. The Last Supper became a sacred and miraculous food by which the believer obtained communion with God and eternal life: in fact, an ever-recurring sacrificial rite. Of all this nothing is to be found in the Gospels themselves. The earthly Jesus did not establish the baptismal rite at all; it was an institution of his community. The Last Supper certainly has its foundation in that most impressive action of Jesus on the evening before his death. But it is not even certain whether by that action Jesus meant to charge his disciples with a rite to be repeated; and the assumption that he instituted thereby a sacrament, a ceremony which, by its outward performance, secured to mankind a supernatural, spiritual good independent of the personal and religious attitude of the believer, contradicts all that we otherwise know of the conduct and character of Jesus. The Gospel of Jesus stands out here in unsurpassed purity, bearing within itself a power which must again and again bring deliverance in spite of all distortion and materialisation. Jesus gave his disciples the spiritual, personal God; to him the personal was everything, the material nothing.

Now this real, living, present and spiritual God was emphatically the Almighty in Jesus' sight. This must not be forgotten, even though we are accustomed to consider other sides of his preaching first. Jesus conceived of God in the whole overwhelming majesty of His being. Even in the fourth Gospel we have "The Father is greater than I."[1] With the fullest and truest human modesty, Jesus

[1] John xiv. 28.

humbled himself before the all-powerful, marvellous, and mysterious God. He strikes a note from the very depths of his soul when he tells his disciples, "Be not afraid of them which kill the body, and after that have no more that they can do. But I will warn you whom ye shall fear: Fear him which, after he hath killed, hath power to cast into hell; yea, I say unto you, Fear him."[1] His own life was swayed by this God whose ways were at times so dark and Himself so hard to recognise. Disappointment after disappointment, suffering upon suffering, did He cast in its path. Nothing was spared to Jesus. After a short and hopeful beginning, there came a standstill and then a rapid retrogression, accompanied by the scorn, contempt, and hostility of all who were of any account in the world, and by the faithlessness of the multitude; then came the clear conviction of the fruitlessness of his work, a foreboding which gradually grew to certainty of his own

[1] Luke xii. 4 f.

dark fate, the dumb impotence of the few who remained true to him, betrayal from the inmost circle of his friends, infinite loneliness and forsakenness, and finally, a death by torture. He learnt that God was terrible, and that an awful darkness and dread encircled Him even for those who stood nearest to Him. How then could this aspect of God have been suppressed in his preaching?

Yet this was, after all, but one side of his faith in God,—one might almost say its hidden substructure. If Jesus had not grasped and proclaimed anything beyond this, he would have been on a level with the great prophets of the Old Testament, or with John the Baptist, but no greater. But the greatest thing about him was that, in spite of his ever-present consciousness of the all-absorbing majesty of God, he yet seized and retained far more surely than any that had gone before him the idea of the inclination of God's nature towards the finite nature of man. Like the rising sun, the faith in God the Father arose and illuminated his preaching. Not that Jesus proclaimed anything absolutely new with such a faith. To the piety of ancient Israel, with its national bias, the belief that God was the Father of Israel and Israel His son had not been unknown. And in the more individualistic piety of later Judaism, the belief occasionally comes to light—and more and more frequently the nearer we approach to Jesus' own time—that God was the Father of each individual believer. These beginnings ought not to be ignored; they represent a religious advance made by later Judaism in this respect, and Jesus was here also the consummator of what already existed. In the piety of the later Hellenic culture, about the time of Jesus and of the infant Church, kindred notes were also struck. Nevertheless the fact remains that the faith in God the Father was nowhere conceived with such unerring certainty, such self-evident simplicity, as in the preaching of Jesus. Jesus created the holiest and most lasting symbol that has ever appeared in the history of religion, the Lord's Prayer, in which all who are truly his disciples will ever meet on common ground. The march of centuries has not been able to rob those parables in which he celebrates the fatherly love of God, of their pristine freshness and truth, for they are fashioned of the finest gold. The glory of the lilies of the field, the joyous song of the birds of the air, the whole world in its beauty bore witness to the fatherly goodness of God. Through his faith in a heavenly Father, a great calm peace broods over the life of Jesus. It is as if, after long erring and straying, our wandering humanity had found its way safely back in Jesus to the living God, and were now taking its rest in silent, long-pent joy.

Jesus' faith in the Fatherhood of God was no shallow optimism. Rather it was an infinitely bold venture. It was his own characteristic achievement that at every moment of his life he could address as *Father* the terrible God who filled his soul with a sense of his unspeakable majesty, and who surrounded his

Jesus' Conception of God   115

whole being with impenetrable darkness and mystery. It was to Him that he turned when the bitter disappointments of his life came upon him: "I thank thee, Father, *Lord of heaven and earth*, that thou didst hide these things from the wise and understanding, and didst reveal them unto babes: yea, Father, for so it was well-pleasing in thy sight."[1] To His will he resigned himself after the bitter struggle in Gethsemane, when disaster stared him in the face: "Father, if it be possible, let this cup pass away from me: nevertheless, not as I will, but as thou wilt." With that great Nevertheless, the property of true faith alone, he spanned the gulf throughout his life between the almighty, unknowable God and our finite humanity. He illuminated the souls of his disciples also with this faith in a heavenly Father. His greatest disciple, Paul, moves us nowhere more powerfully and deeply than when, following wholly in the spirit and on the lines of the Gospel, he speaks of the

[1] Matt. xi. 25.

believers' sonship to God, of the Spirit who bears witness that we are the sons of God. The eighth chapter of Romans, especially the second half, is like a splendid fugue on the theme of the Fatherhood of God: "If God is for us, who is against us?" When Paul strikes the keynote of joy in his epistles—"Rejoice alway, and again I say unto you, Rejoice"—when he glories in the sufferings he has undergone, when in the New Testament writings it is so often the παρρησία, the glad, free, confident courage that is extolled as the chief virtue of the Christians, all this is but the strong expression of the faith in a heavenly Father which Jesus awakened in the hearts of his disciples.

CHAPTER VII

The Last Judgment

Such was the preaching of Jesus and his faith in God as seen in its kindly aspect. But all this has a reverse side. The single word in which the tradition summed up his preaching was, "*Repent ye*, for the kingdom of heaven is at hand."[1] The idea of the Kingdom of God is directly connected in Jesus' mind with that of the Last Judgment. When God came, it would be to judge the world. Therefore his preaching of the Kingdom had not only its benevolent, consolatory side, but also made stern and exacting demands: Repent ye, alter your whole frame of mind, that ye may stand before God when He cometh.

[1] Matt. iv. 17.

With the idea of the Judgment Jesus again comes into close and direct contact with the religious feelings and conceptions of his time and environment. Here too the later Jewish piety had prepared the field for the Gospel. The idea of God's Judgment had been the central point of the prophetic utterances, whether it was expected upon Israel and what was evil and rotten in Israel, or upon the enemies of the moment. It had undergone an enormous extension during the later development of Jewish faith. The idea of a *world-*judgment had gradually formed itself, for Israel's arch-foe at the time of Jesus was of course the world-empire of Rome, so that any judgment upon that empire must become a judgment upon all the nations of the earth. Yet not only the nations should be judged, according to this later Judaistic conception, but all the hostile powers at work in this world, the demons, and at their head that great antagonist of God, the Devil; and not only upon the present generation should God's judgment

The Last Judgment

fall, but the dead should rise to receive their sentences, and these mighty events should be accomplished amid tremendous cataclysms of the heavens and the earth. These ideas lay deep in the heart of every pious Israelite, and again and again do we find references in later Jewish literature to the great and terrible Day of the Lord, the last grand Judgment. And each man had in his mind's eye the majestic image of the Judge, as it had once been drawn by the author of the Book of Daniel: the Ancient of Days, with snow-white hair, sitting surrounded by hosts of angels upon a throne from which streams of fire gushed forth. Yet this Jewish idea of the Judgment was subject to one important limitation: it remained entirely national. However widely it was extended in all directions, its central core was still formed by the hope that the world-power hostile to Israel would be annihilated and the faithful Israel reinstated in his rights. It is true that among the devout the expectation of a judgment upon the godless section of their own people occupied a foremost place. The devout felt themselves to be only a part of the nation—and indeed usually the weakest part,—yet they alone should come to their rights at the Judgment, while the rest should have *judgment* only. But here it was merely the fanaticism of a sect or a party that had taken the place of, or rather ranged itself beside, the national hopes and passions. In the eschatological reflections of Israel it is always a case of "the godly" or "the godless" as a class; the individual does not place himself alone and naked before the idea of the Judgment, but shelters himself behind the group to which he belongs, or reassures himself by the consciousness that he is one with his sect. The prevailing instinct among pious Israelites is the corporate one of the "nine-and-ninety righteous men,"—that feeling which the Baptist had already scourged: "Begin not to say within yourselves, We have Abraham for our father; for I say unto you that God is able of these stones to raise up children unto Abraham."

The Last Judgment

Now there can be no doubt that Jesus adopted the more advanced ideas of later Judaism. Like the rest of his time, he looked for the final judgment of God upon the whole world, that is, upon all the nations and upon the Devil and his hosts; he looked for the resurrection of the dead and the great decision of Heaven or Hell for all. In all these matters, however, he showed an unusual reserve, and he never gave any connected picture of his own conception of the end of the world and of the Judgment. The great majority of the prophecies in the thirteenth chapter of Mark and its parallels are probably only the product of the Christian community, as is also the great parable of the Son of Man separating all the nations before his throne to the right hand and to the left.[1] It was contrary to his inmost nature to give such a detailed picture in all its stages of the events of the Last Day; he was no painter of the colossal. He protested against the pre-

[1] Matt. xxv. 31 ff.

tensions and the efforts of Jewish apocalyptics to calculate the end by the signs of the times. No man could tell the day and hour: the coming of the Kingdom was not to be reckoned beforehand. Indeed he lays all his emphasis upon the sudden coming of the end. It would come like a thief in the night,[1] like a destroying flood, like the judgment in the time of Noah and of Lot, like the lightning flashing across the heavens.[2] Therefore all disciples of Jesus must be true and wakeful at all moments. They must stand ready with loins girded and lamps burning,[3] for the Lord may come at any hour of the night. In other respects too he shows a remarkably sober restraint in his description of the last things, especially in that of the respective conditions of the godly and the godless after God's Judgment. With a few brief strokes he indicates the essential points, but only so far as they may serve to impress upon his disciples and hearers the importance

---

[1] Matt. xxiv. 43 ff.; Luke xvii. 26 ff.
[2] Luke xvii. 24.   [3] Luke xii. 35 f.

The Last Judgment

of the great decision. In many points of detail we are left quite in the dark as to his real views. We do not even know, for instance, whether he presupposed a general resurrection of the dead or merely a resurrection of the righteous.[1] When we compare Jesus' utterances concerning the Last Things with the broad scene-painting of Jewish apocalyptics, or the discourses of Mahomet, with their repulsive descriptions of heaven and hell, there rises before our eyes a conviction of the serene greatness, moral and religious, and the clearness and earnestness of such a mind, which could confine itself so closely to the absolutely needful.

While, however, Jesus' preaching was thus based, generally speaking, on the ideas of the Judgment as developed by later Judaism, in one point he goes decidedly beyond them, purifying, illuminating, and exalting them. For as he detached the idea of the Kingdom of God from the nation and the national hopes,

[1] The latter view is supported by Luke xiv. 14, xx. 36.

so at the same time he detached the idea of the Judgment. What Jewish eschatology had made the principal point—the judging of the enemies of Israel and Israel's recovery of lost rights—plays no part whatever in Jesus' preaching of the Judgment. More than this, he broke with the corporate instinct of his devout contemporaries. With resolute determination and inexorable clearness he set the individual in the place of the nation, the party, or the sect. In justice to the righteous, it ought certainly to be borne in mind that even the Jewish legalists had not wholly lost sight of the conviction that the ultimate Judgment of God would be concerned with the individual and the individual alone. Here and there among them the individualistic note is struck clearly enough. But these isolated notes are lost in the general battle-cry of "Israel here, the Gentiles there: the righteous here, the godless there!" With unrivalled energy, on the other hand, Jesus forced the opposite conviction upon the souls of his disciples:

The Last Judgment

All depends upon you individually, he cried, and upon you alone. You must render your account before the living God; there is nothing behind which you can shelter and conceal yourself. Two men shall be lying on one bed: the one shall be accepted, the other cast aside. Two women shall be grinding at one mill: the one shall be accepted, the other cast aside.[1] The one sinner who turns and repents is worth more in the sight of God than the whole herd of the righteous.[2] The individual possesses in his life—which he must keep pure against the Judgment of God—a treasure compared to which all the treasures of this world do not weigh in the balance.[3] How the individual has traded with the talent entrusted to him will be the test before God's searching eyes.[4]

Now this is the point at which the religious line in the preaching of Jesus meets the ethical. For the thing which gives value to the indi-

---

[1] Luke xvii. 34 f.   [2] Luke xv. 7, 10.
[3] Mark viii. 36.   [4] Matt. xxv. 14 ff.

vidual on his trial before the eyes of God is simply and solely his moral good. God is good, and therefore they who would find Him must seek Him in the good. Thus the ethical demands of Jesus are based entirely upon the idea of the Judgment. Whether expressed or not, there lies in reality behind all his moral exhortations the idea that man will have to answer for his deeds before God's great tribunal. He alone is to be feared, the God who has power to cast into Hell, but not any of His creatures. He alone must also be obeyed.

The knowledge that all Jesus' moral demands were based upon and prompted by the idea of reward and punishment in the Last Judgment ought not to frighten us. It is true that we often hear it laid down from the standpoint of Kantian rigorism that the ethics of Jesus stand on a lower plane because of their prevailing idea of reward, that in fact they are "eudæmonistic." In any case, however, they are very far removed from the

The Last Judgment

really dangerous, sensual eudæmonism which consists in measuring the value of ethical actions by the standard of ordinary utility or of sensual pleasure. Jesus' ultimate conception of reward and punishment was one pre-eminently spiritual, supersensual, and ideal. The reward he preaches is, virtually speaking, existence in the sight of God, nearness to God, and the punishment, rejection by God, removal from His presence. All else that he occasionally speaks of—the joys of Heaven or the torments of Hell—belongs to the easily detachable form or shell. The man to whom the so-called eudæmonistic foundation of Jesus' moral demands will appeal at all, must indeed be one who already lives in the supersensual and the ideal, in a world beyond the ordinary utility of the day, and the pleasures, more or less refined, of the senses. And if that is so, the reward of the Gospel will not be to him a mere outward remuneration, but an inward acceptance and recognition, an encouragement and confirmation in what he already has; it will be a spiritual necessity. Moreover, Jesus saved the Gospel idea of reward from the special danger by which Pharisaism was beset—the spirit of bargaining and haggling with God and of boastful reliance on one's own merit. In the easiest and simplest way he combines the idea of reward with the overwhelming consciousness of the divine goodness and mercy. The servant who had done all that was commanded him[1] had yet only done his duty; he had no claim on any recompense, or on the personal gratitude of his Lord. If the all-powerful God gives Himself in blessed nearness to those of His children who have served Him faithfully, that in itself is an overflowing and all-sufficient good, to which man cannot lay claim as his just reward. When we have done all, let us still say: We are servants. We can but admire the infinite clearness and certainty with which Jesus here surmounted the dangers of the Pharisaic ethics of reward,—far more

[1] Luke xvii. 7 ff.

surely and simply indeed than Paul, with all the ingenious proofs by which he sought to defend his doctrine of justification by faith alone.

Nevertheless we must learn to accept the fact that the Gospel knows nothing of the doctrine that man ought to do good for its own sake. What the Gospel constantly repeats is: Do good for God's sake, do good for the sake of the eternal goal which God has set you, and in the ever-present sense of responsibility before the great tribunal in which God will cast the final balance of your life. In the very heart of the Gospel lies, not the bloodless image of the moral law, but the immovable conviction that the individual personal life has its goal and its consummation in God.

CHAPTER VIII

The Moral Teaching of Jesus

WE have now to ask, What was the essential content and the fundamental character of the moral demands of Jesus? The devout Jew of Jesus' time found the substance of God's will in the Mosaic law. Put with greater definiteness, then, the question runs: What attitude did Jesus take up towards the Mosaic law? The view that here too he identified himself at first wholly with the feelings of the past is quite consistent with the position he adopted towards the national hopes of his day, the ideas of the Kingdom of God and of the Judgment. There can be no doubt that Jesus accepted the sacred will of God as embodied in the law with genuine conviction. To the

The Moral Teaching of Jesus 131

Scribe who asked him what he should do to inherit eternal life, he answered: "What is written in the law? How readest thou?" And then: "This do, and thou shalt live."[1] In the law he found the good and holy will of God. It is true that he once said, "Except your righteousness exceed the righteousness of the Scribes and Pharisees, ye cannot enter into the kingdom of Heaven";[2] but he considered that these had falsified, defaced, and defiled the holy Will of God by their tradition.[3] He contended first and foremost for the Mosaic law and the Old Testament against the tradition, against what was "said to them of old time."[4] Nor can it be disproved that Jesus, as the tradition reports, and possibly in opposition to the thoughtless worldlings who pressed around him, uttered the words, "Think ye that I came to destroy the law and the

[1] Luke x. 25–28, and *cf.* Mark x. 17 ff.
[2] Matt v. 20.
[3] Mark vii. 6 ff.
[4] Matt. v. 21, etc.

prophets? I came not to destroy, but to fulfil."¹

On a closer examination, however, a deep gulf is observed between the law itself, product and growth of the period of declining piety in Israel, and the spirit of Jesus' moral precepts. Seen by the light of day, Jesus' belief that he rested on a foundation of the law is in much the same case as Luther's, that he was still a faithful son of the Catholic Church when he had inwardly long broken with her. Jesus believed that in his battle with the fundamental moral ideas of the Scribes and Pharisees he was only striking at the tradition and its ramifications. In reality, however, he was striking at the law, upon which not he, but his Pharisaic opponents, actually based themselves. And in the heat of battle the deeper antagonism did occasionally reveal itself. In most of the great anti-

---

[1] Matt. v. 17. These words, however, can scarcely have stood traditionally at the beginning of the great "Sermon on the Mount." They are an isolated paradoxical logion, such as Luke xvi. 16 f.

The Moral Teaching of Jesus   133

theses of the Sermon on the Mount it certainly seems as if he were aiming not at the law, but only at the tradition of his opponents. But when Jesus opposed the commandment of "an eye for an eye and a tooth for a tooth" with the commandment of unqualified non-resistance and forgiveness,[1] it became manifest that the spirit of the "higher righteousness" was different in kind from that of the Mosaic law, or at least of a part of it. When he insisted so strongly upon the indissolubility of marriage, he overrode a provision of the law concerning divorce, of extreme importance to the Scribes.[2] When he announced that the Sabbath was made for man, and not man for the Sabbath,[3] he threw over at least one side of the Old Testament conception of the Sabbath.[4] And still more when he uttered

---

[1] Matt. v. 38 ff.
[2] Mark x. 2 f.; Matt. v. 31.   [3] Mark ii. 27.
[4] This view is not altered by the fact that the rabbinic doctors themselves occasionally made use of this principle by way of justification in their casuistic treatment of the law.

the hard saying which even his disciples thought a bold paradox, that nothing from without the man going into him could defile him,[1] a whole revolution was implied against the cleansing ordinances of the Old Testament. The freedom with which Jesus treated the details of the Mosaic law, while humbly bowing to it as a whole, is perhaps best shown by his challenging dictum on divorce. The view he expresses certainly comes into conflict with a particular ordinance of the Mosaic law; that he fully acknowledges. But, he declares, Moses only made that ordinance because of the people's hardness of heart, and higher than the authority of Moses himself stood the authority of God the Creator, who ordained the indissolubility of marriage. Bold indeed would have been the Scribe who ventured on such an argument!

We find, then, that Jesus' attitude towards the law was paradoxical; for with all his inward freedom he maintained towards it an

[1] Mark vii. 14 ff.

The Moral Teaching of Jesus

attitude of reverent humility, and with all his differences in detail, he clung firmly to his agreement with it as a whole. The law was and remained to him the holy Will of God, but he heard in it only those notes to which his ear was attuned.

In these circumstances the moral ideas peculiar to Jesus will be more clearly perceptible if we consider, not the position he took up towards the law, but the struggle he maintained against what he himself sharply distinguished from it—the legal tradition. "Except your righteousness exceed the righteousness of the Scribes and Pharisees, ye cannot enter into the kingdom of heaven." In what, then, did this higher righteousness consist? First and foremost, in concentration upon the genuinely moral. Both Jesus and his opponents started from the holy Will of God as laid down in the Mosaic law. Yet how differently did they conceive it! The Scribes and Pharisees wanted the "whole" law, with all its ritual and ceremonial, its juristic and constitutional ordinances. Of course they wanted the moral side of it also, but only in addition to a great deal else. And naturally the moral side came off the loser. Jesus' soul, on the other hand, was filled only with the majesty of the moral law; the rest he passed by with indifference. He did not attack it; he left it where it was. Only when these non-essentials threatened to hamper the essential, he rose and struck down the rotten trash. Then he entered the lists on behalf of the inward purity before the outward, of right-doing before Sabbath-keeping, of filial love before sacrifice, of righteousness, mercy, and truth before the tithe.[1] Thus from the centre outwards he accomplished the liberation of the moral element in the law from its accretions.

And with all this he insisted upon unity, completeness, and reality. From the infinite subdivision of the commandments of God in the law, he led his hearers back to unity;

[1] Matt. xxiii. 23.

The Moral Teaching of Jesus 137

instead of the bewildering confusion of the legal atmosphere, with its medley of great and small, important and unimportant, he gave them a *whole*. "Thou shalt love the Lord thy God with all thy heart, and thy neighbour as thyself."[1] "Whatsoever ye would that men should do unto you, even so do ye also unto them."[2] The point is not that Jesus should once have uttered and laid down these principles. Similar sayings may be met with here and there among his rabbinic contemporaries, and Jews and Judaists declare with pride that Jesus here taught nothing new. What matters is the vital energy, the unique certainty, with which Jesus actually regulated his own and his disciples' lives. Nowhere did he tolerate a superficial juggling with the words and commandments of God; he was constantly setting his disciples before the ultimate moral realities, and constantly insisting upon the personal element and upon that which gave its true value to life, the love of God, expressing

[1] Mark xii. 28 ff.   [2] Matt. vii. 12.

itself in the love of neighbour and of brother, and in duty towards that self[1] which was of more value than all the world.

The law as interpreted by Pharisaism was by its whole nature directed to the individual action. This later Jewish law was in fact also common law, and common law is of necessity concerned with the individual action. Such a combination of law, morality, and religion is characteristic of the mental attitude of Judaism. What Jesus did was to separate them. He presses behind the individual action to the *disposition*: "Make the tree good, and its fruit also will be good."[2] Out of the abundance of the heart, he declared, come the pure thoughts as well as those which defile the man.[3] Personal freedom, resting on moral conviction. takes the place of all the mass of casuistic, soul-fettering commandments. According to a tradition preserved in an early manuscript of Luke's Gospel, Jesus is made

---
[1] He says, "Love thy neighbour *as thyself*."
[2] Matt. xii. 33.   [3] Matt. xii. 35; Mark vii. 21 ff.

to say to a man who was working on the Sabbath: "If thou knowest what thou doest, blessed art thou; but if thou knowest not, thou art accursed and a transgressor of the law."[1] There is little reason to doubt that Jesus uttered this bold word, which would then have its echo in the Pauline phrase, "Whatsoever is not of faith (*i.e.* of moral conviction) is sin."[2] But whether it is his or not, his whole life and his whole person are an embodiment of freedom based on moral conviction.

In this struggle against Pharisaism on behalf of the unity, completeness, inwardness, and freedom of all moral effort, Jesus was swayed by one strong fundamental feeling—his passion for truth and reality. Not only a subjective love of truth inspired him, but an instinctive feeling for the practical and the real. Hence his invincible dislike of all conscious and unconscious artificiality, of all clinging to the superficial, the external, and the purposeless, of

[1] In Codex D, at Luke vi. 4. [2] Rom. xiv. 23.

all that was in reality mere trifling under the mask of earnestness. In his gentle compassion there was much that he could understand and forgive, but when he lit upon these things, his wrath flamed up: he could have no fellowship with them, for he saw that they were rotten to the core. And so hard did he hit his opponents, that to-day we can almost feel pity for them. There were but few conscious impostors among them; in their way they all meant it seriously. "I bear them witness that they have a zeal for God, but not according to knowledge," cries their former greatest partisan.[1] On the other hand, Jesus had no choice but to contend with fervour against a system which had unnerved its votaries and deprived them of the sense of reality. For where that is lost, all is lost; God dwells in the real, and he who has lost his sense of the real will not find God. Thus in his war against the Scribes and Pharisees Jesus appears as the great champion of truth and reality.

[1] Rom. x. 2.

The Moral Teaching of Jesus 141

Still deeper than this conscious antagonism, however, between Jesus and Pharisaism, lies what may rather be called the unconscious and the unexpressed. We have already said that the special characteristic of the ethics and religion of later Judaism was their intimate connection with *law*. The relation between God and the righteous, the righteous and his neighbour, is here calculated on a legal basis to the last detail, in a system of actions and counter-actions. The sober, commonplace and common-sense view of *ne quid nimis* is the dominant principle. Everything is minutely weighed and measured in a casuistic plan which extends to the most trivial cases of ordinary life. The negative spirit of prohibition, the "Thou shalt not," is everywhere in the ascendant, and the dignity of morality in its positive form, endlessly driving man beyond and outside himself, is never recognised.

We can only obtain the proper insight into Jesus' moral atmosphere when we realise that he pressed in the opposite direction to Pharisaism in partially unconscious antagonism to it, and, let us frankly confess, to the length of uncompromising one-sidedness. What he preached was the ethics of heroism, of absolute, unquestioning enthusiasm. Only from this point of view can we understand the spirit of the Sermon on the Mount, which his pious followers put together out of his sayings.

We can now understand, too, why Jesus would have nothing to say to ordinary law and the legal point of view. His whole nature was set to higher things. To the legal principle of the Old Testament, "An eye for an eye and a tooth for a tooth," he opposed the commandment not to resist evil in any circumstances. To the young man who appeals to him in his dispute with his brother, he replies with a stern refusal.[1] When Jesus saved the woman taken in adultery [2] from popular justice,

[1] Luke xii. 13 f.
[2] John vii. 53–viii. 11. According to our best manuscripts, this passage about the woman taken in adultery did not originally stand here. It is a piece of genuine but extra-canonical tradition.

The Moral Teaching of Jesus 143

by appealing to the highest moral standards, we can clearly perceive, in spite of our admiration for the grandeur of the scene, that his magnificent and unbounded moral one-sidedness did constitute a danger to the maintenance of law and order. It is the clash of two worlds whose limits will not always be easy to define. But what Jesus had to do was to break a passage for the higher moral view, to liberate this higher world from the lower one of every day. And there even one-sidedness may be in season.

The antagonism between the deeper moral conceptions of Jesus and the legal and casuistic world of the Pharisees is amply illustrated by the splendid irony with which he occasionally imitates their manner in his own maxims: "I say unto you that every one who is angry with his brother shall be in danger of the judgment (or petty tribunal), and whosoever shall say to his brother "Raca," shall be in danger of the council (or higher tribunal); and whosoever shall say "Thou fool," shall be in danger of the hell of fire."¹ We can see now why Jesus was so fond of laying down the commandment of God in all its absoluteness in the face of this endless system of distinctions and exceptions. To one who has studied the Pharisaic casuistry of oaths and marriage, it will not be surprising that Jesus demanded, in his heroic manner, that swearing should be altogether eschewed, and that marriage should never and in no circumstances be dissolved.² The enlightened and sensible interpretation certainly is that there might still be ultimate exceptions, and that Jesus himself occasionally made an exception, *e.g.* in the case of his prohibition of swearing. But Jesus hated exceptions; placed as he was, he was bound to fight hard for the inviolable earnestness of the moral view, whose existence was endangered by the quibbles of the law.

The ethics of Pharisaism are embodied in

¹ Matt. v. 22.

² The words, "except for adultery," Matt. v. 32, are an interpolation; *cf.* Mark x. 11 ff., Matt. xix. 1 ff., Luke xvi. 18. They are inconsistent with the absolute tone of Jesus' ethics.

The Moral Teaching of Jesus 145

prohibition and in the exact limitation of the moral law. Jesus' whole tone is positive; he tells his disciples what they are to do, and he is fond of awakening their souls to the unlimited vastness of the moral law. If the Jewish commandment ran: "Whatsoever ye would that men should not do unto you, do it not unto them," Jesus said: "Whatsoever ye would that men should do unto you, do it also unto them." Though this difference may at first sight seem insignificant, we are justified in paying it some attention. The Jewish commandment lies in the province of calm and reasonable reflection, whereas the moral world of Jesus, as revealed in his sayings, becomes absolutely limitless. He continually lays stress upon the unboundedness of the moral obligation. It is not enough to forgive one's brother seven times: it must be seventy times seven.[1] The commandment knows no limits; these duties must be fulfilled at once, without thought or hesitation, without "if" or "but."

[1] Matt. xviii. 21 ff.

The morally perfect man must allow nothing to stand in the way, not even the so-called service of God.[1] And as Jesus extends our obligations into the scale of the infinite, so on the other hand he pursues them into their minutest details of word and disposition, in both directions opening up an immeasurable field. When he speaks of his disciples' duty towards themselves, it is the same thing over again. Everything must be sacrificed in order not to lose *oneself*. Even a part of that self should be forfeited, hand or foot cut off or an eye plucked out, in order to enter into the Kingdom of God.[2] All values in the world cannot outweigh man's proper self. In short, the infinitude of Jesus' moral ideal may best be summed up in the saying, "Be ye therefore perfect, even as your heavenly Father is perfect."[3] An inconceivably bold demand, filling our souls with dismay. Man the finite is to direct his strivings towards becoming

---

[1] Matt. v. 23 f.; Mark xi. 25.
[2] Mark ix. 43, 47; Matt. v. 29 f.   [3] Matt. v. 48.

perfect as the eternal and infinite God, and by his strong and unerring moral power he is to enable himself to smile at all obstacles and provocations, and even to love his adversary and to treat him with kindness. In this sphere of highest and divinest enthusiasm, filled with God's spirit and pressing on into the very presence of God, lies the commandment to "love your enemies."[1]

Heroism, enthusiasm—here was the keynote of Jesus' morality. It meant a boundless devotion to the sacred Will of God, which knew neither condition nor exception, and was continually urging man on from task to task and leaving him no rest; it meant the forcible liberation of the moral element from all the ignobler things which had twined themselves almost indissolubly around it, and the final extrication of the moral law in all its sternness and majesty. When Paul represented the moral life of the Christian as the work of the miraculous Spirit of God ever driving him

[1] Matt. v. 44 f.

on, he had found an excellent formula for the very essence of Jesus' moral teaching. For to act morally *is* to act heroically, in the rush of enthusiasm and under the stress of a divine power not our own.

The effect of it all is, moreover, greatly strengthened by the eschatological colour of his preaching. The last links of the chain here fall into their place. We have seen that the great idea of the Judgment was the foundation of his moral demands. The Judgment is at hand, he cried, God is at hand. It was because he felt so unshakably convinced of the advent of God that there existed for him no other reality than that of this infinite and holy Will of God, which held the soul of man in trembling unrest, and to which all quibbling was hateful. That was why he cried, " Repent ye, for the kingdom of God is at hand." Wherever he turned he saw that a moral upheaval from the very foundations, a complete liberation from the inferior and the trivial, and a mighty aspiration towards

The Moral Teaching of Jesus

the newly opened realms of the divine Will were the first necessities if God were not to come with destruction in His hand.

It may be seen from the foregoing that a mere plain statement of the moral ideas of Jesus is an impossibility. We must recognise that he stands in a wholly unique position, that in that position God gave him something wholly unique to say, and that he said it in all its nakedness and its terrible earnest. To endeavour to imitate him in every detail would be a presumptuous enterprise, an attempt of the ordinary man to measure himself against the hero. He is, and must remain, beyond our reach.

In one aspect, indeed, the moral world of Jesus seems to us strange, and appears to show some flaw. In all his moral demands his gaze is directed exclusively towards God and the individual. The subsistence of the individual before God's tribunal is the point which alone seems to be of any importance in his eyes. His ethics are the ethics of lofty individualism. Beside these two entities of God and the individual everything else sinks into the background. No account is taken of the history of man as a whole or of the connected labour of the human race in the wider or narrower forms of its social life—marriage, the family, society, the state, the nation. Jesus makes his moral demands as if the individual stood free and naked before God, absolved from all these relationships and customary standards—except as regards the direct relationship of man to man,—as in fact Jesus and his disciples in their wandering life lived free from all such forms and relationships. And in addition to this we have Jesus' expectation of an approaching millennium, or at least of a great disruption of all existing circumstances. The whole labour of the world in the nation, the state and the forms of legal and social life, the labour in which generation succeeds generation like the links in a chain, was to him incapable of producing anything more of permanent value. Nor should it be forgotten

The Moral Teaching of Jesus 151

that Jesus grew up far removed from any real culture, among a ruined and hopeless people utterly deprived of all great aims. The actual roots of his anti-worldly ethics do not perhaps lie there; the lofty, individualistic morality of Jesus had, as we have seen, its own roots and would still have existed if he had grown up among other outward circumstances and with other expectations; for such a purely religious and unworldly view of things is quite conceivable even when detached from these particular conditions. But they certainly served to encourage that fundamental bias of Jesus' moral nature; they provided the form, exclusively religious and anti-worldly, in which it slowly moulded itself.

Here and there, no doubt, Jesus gave his attention to various sides of the social life of men, sometimes even directly attacking or abrogating them. He spoke golden words on the inviolability and sacredness of marriage. His eye kindled, grave and other-worldly as he was, at the sight of children. His saying,

"Render unto Cæsar the things that are Cæsar's, and unto God the things that are God's," has gone through the centuries making the history of man. Nevertheless these are details, crumbs that fall from the rich man's table, and no one will seriously assert that the strongest side of his moral work lay here. Considered as a whole, Jesus absolved both himself and his disciples from the life of marriage, the family, and the profession, and only poured forth the full treasures of his personality when released from such conditions. He forbade all care for the morrow, and not only restless, untrusting care, but all kinds of calculation and planning beforehand, which are necessary to every worldly calling on a larger scale.[1] Wealth he held to be at the very least fraught with danger to the soul.[2] As we have already seen, he would never have much to do with law, even in its proper place. He lived in an atmosphere where law frequently meant

[1] Matt. vi. 19 ff., esp. ver. 34.   [2] Mark x. 23 ff.

The Moral Teaching of Jesus 153

nothing but force and oppression, and where his fellow-countrymen were on the whole glad to have as few dealings with the law and its courts as possible. The government was, in his eyes, a power belonging to this world, to which one owed obedience so long as one had dealings with the world. But regarded from the highest point of view, it was morally of little value. "The kings of the Gentiles have lordship over them, and their oppressors are called benefactors!"[1] He separated his hopes and his faith from the thought of his people's doom; he stared the terrible certainty of their destruction in the face, and fled for refuge to a higher atmosphere, while this world and its labour, even the labour devoted to loftier aims, faded into oblivion beside his soul's thirst after God.

We are bound to recognise these facts, and to acknowledge freely that in this respect we can no longer simply imitate and endorse the

[1] Luke xxii. 25: another instance of irony in the sayings of Jesus.

practice of Jesus. The progress of events—to submit to which is also part of the service of God, since God is manifested in it—has brought the labour of the world and the discharge of its tasks very near to us as a moral duty, nay, has forced it upon us. The evolution of Christianity has followed in its wake, and it is through the Reformation and the act of Luther that a glad, confident appreciation of the labour of the world in its moral aspect has again been made possible to us. We no longer live in imagination at the latter end of a decaying world. The supersensual realm of God, with its eternal ideas, has grown into and around this finite world-labour of ours in ways that were quite unknown to the age of Jesus. The boundaries of the world and the Kingdom of God have become subtler, vaguer, and more fluid.

But when this is said, has the whole moral attitude of Jesus little or nothing left to give us? On the contrary, it has the ultimate and highest gift. Jesus tells us what is, after all,

The Moral Teaching of Jesus

the fundamental, vital thing amid all our confused toilings: that the individual or individuals *can* find the living God, that the individual must lead his life under an earnest sense of responsibility before the great eyes of God, free from all thought of outward success and unfettered by the judgment of men; that he must find his stay and support in the strong and beneficent Will of God, as well as his guarantee for the freedom and independence of his personality in the midst of this world's toil; that he exists here on earth only in order to become fitted for eternity. If Jesus sought this ultimate goal and impressed it on the souls of his disciples while standing outside the ordinary course of the world, he may seem to us strange and inaccessible in this latter respect, but all the more clearly does he hold up the mark towards which our lives are bound to strive even within the limits of our worldly labour.

But, it may be said, does not a deep gulf still yawn between our life, encompassed as it is by the affairs of this world and devoted to culture or to professional work, and the anti-worldly practice of Jesus and his first disciples; so that the question would again arise whether the community of ultimate aim could be maintained in spite of these fundamental differences? I do not think so. These two different worlds meet at any rate in one point. Jesus continually emphasised as distinctly as it is possible to do so the root idea that the individual only grows and matures through human intercourse, without which there can be no highest life, and that God Himself is only to be found in the love of one's neighbour and the moral effort which that love entails. With the same energy with which he directed the souls of his disciples towards God, he directed them towards personal intercourse; he did not, like Buddha, throw them back finally upon themselves, but bound them in close, lasting, and intimate communion with himself and one another. And since he insisted that the highest good

The Moral Teaching of Jesus 157

lay in moral work in the community which he wove between person and person, it is inevitable that all the necessary forms of the social life of man should gradually be reestablished, nay, should for the first time be rated at their true value. The Gospel, the moral teaching of Jesus, does not lead to the cloister doors, like the religion of Buddha; ultimately it must surely approve the forms of human society, because it approves with its whole being the moral forces which the latter brings to light.

Thus Jesus finally reveals to us by his teaching the true and ultimate Will of God. In his heroic stature and his absolute self-devotion, in his exclusive insistence upon the highest and the best and his scorning of anything less, he stands perhaps at an unattainable distance from us, and even shows an unbending sternness, nay, an awfulness before which we shrink. We cannot presume to measure ourselves against the hero. Yet he remains the conscience of his followers; his words are still the thorn which allows them no rest. With unwavering clearness he points out the way which we must follow, even if he himself is far beyond our reach.

Yet the sternness and earnestness of Jesus' moral demands have a reverse side, without which he and his preaching might indeed be called terrible: he proclaimed the forgiveness of sins and a sin-forgiving God. He did not only lay upon his disciples the heavy burden of his moral exactions, but taught them also to pray daily, "Father, forgive us our trespasses." Contemporary Judaism is also possessed with this idea of the forgiveness of sin and debt. "Forgive us, O our Father, for we have sinned; forgive us, O our King, for we have done wrong,"—so prayed the pious Israelite day by day, perhaps already at the time of Jesus, certainly soon afterwards. Later Jewish literature is full of prayers of repentance and confessions of sin which are often moving and beautiful. And yet their writers could never become truly sure and confident of their sin-forgiving God. All the artificial striving of the law, with its heaping-up of externals round true piety, bears witness to the contrary. And how indeed could any-one have had faith in such a sin-forgiving, merciful God when he himself was practising for religion's sake unmercifulness, unforgiving-ness, and forgetfulness towards his neighbour? In proportion as the pious Jew's longing for the forgiveness of sins found freer and freer expression, he yielded more and more com-pletely to the tendency towards exclusiveness and towards a haughty contempt and hatred of all who were not as he was. He despised the Greeks and hated the Romans, he lived in a state of bloody feud with the Samaritans, and extended his enmity and hatred to all Israelites who, from whatever grounds, did not share his isolation—viz., the sinners and godless who had dealings with the Gentiles, and the publicans who made their living out of the blood-money which enriched the pagan over-lords. The Pharisee hated and despised the

"Amhaarez"—the uneducated common folk who could not read and study the Scriptures, and could not therefore apply themselves seriously to the fulfilment of the law—and held himself scrupulously aloof from any contact with them. Now Jesus immediately took up a line of decided and refreshing opposition to this whole tendency. Even the popular verdict recognised in this respect the unwonted and peculiar manner of Jesus: "He eats with publicans and sinners," cried the multitude.[1] He made no advances to the party of devout exclusiveness, but went from the very first among the despised and uneducated masses, among the publicans and sinners, the children of this world, whom good society had spurned and cast out and given up for lost. The Gospels also tell us that he was friendly to the Samaritans,[2] and he has certainly raised them an undying monument in one of his finest parables.[3] All this he did quite

---

[1] Matt. xi. 19.
[2] Luke ix. 51 ff.; xvii. 11 ff.   [3] Luke x. 30 ff.

naturally and of his own free will, as though it could not be otherwise. Far from the streets and the high-roads, where the herd of the pious took their way, Jesus went about seeking the lost and strayed who had no power to right themselves. And even when he came across wholly lost and fallen souls—a prostitute or an adulterous wife—he turned to them with gentle kindness. He could do so without relaxing the earnestness of his moral tone, because he was strong, and because no impure atmosphere was capable of sullying his purity. Here indeed he won his proudest triumphs. The most wonderful thing about him was, after all, that he who made such stern, serious, and austere demands upon his disciples could be so full of mercy and of womanly kindness when he found a human soul impotently wrestling with sin. He in whose sight no man could do enough was content with the first weak signs of the right will; he who set so infinitely high a standard could take pleasure in the first stumbling steps made on the unwonted road. He came to cast fire on the earth, and he rejoiced in each faint spark of the divine that gleamed up in a human soul. Hence it was that he could grasp with fullest confidence the idea of the sin-forgiving God, and could implant the same confidence in the souls of His disciples. Here at last his preaching touches its climax. In the loveliest of his parables, which have gone down the ages in undying freshness, exerting their unbroken influence on the souls of a battling humanity, Jesus celebrated this sin-forgiving God, now as the father who receives his lost son with strong, unwavering love and even with rejoicing, and now as the almighty God in whose eyes the one sinner who repents is worth more than the nine-and-ninety righteous who need no repentance. *Thus the Gospel becomes the religion of ethical liberation, for in its very centre lies the belief in the release and unfettering of the will for good by the forgiveness of sins.*

Jesus was, moreover, quite conscious of the fact that this faith in a sin-forgiving God must go hand in hand with man's general moral conduct, and indeed could not exist without it. "Forgive us our trespasses, even as we forgive them that trespass against us." In oft-repeated phrases Jesus made it clear to his disciples that only the merciful could have faith in a merciful Father, and that belief in a sin-forgiving God was impossible to a hard and unforgiving heart.[1]

Finally, let us observe once more the root characteristic of the message of Jesus, expressing itself so constantly here and elsewhere. Let us observe how intimately and in what mutual dependence the moral and the religious are interwoven throughout his preaching. His faith becomes inconceivable detached from his morality, and conversely the latter is only conceivable on the ground of his faith. The religious and moral forces are intertwined in endless harmony; a freed religion and a freed

[1] Matt. v. 7, vi. 14 f., vii. 1 ff., xviii. 23 ff.; Mark xi. 25.

morality join in indissoluble alliance and flow on in one strong, united stream. Both, however, find their ultimate goal in the personal relation. The Gospel was in the highest and most perfect sense a personal religion. Everything in it is concerned with the personal and the spiritual. Its central point is faith in the living God, who holds communion with man only through the spiritual and personal, never through the material. Jesus' detachment of religion from the nation and the national hopes means simply that the individual, *i.e.* the moral personality, now assumes the position of paramount importance. Jesus regarded the Judgment no longer as a judgment upon certain nations, parties, and sects, but upon the individual. The life of the individual, placed directly before God's tribunal and burdened with an immense responsibility, gains an eternal and immeasurable significance. Jesus' moral requirements too, freed from all complications of cult and ceremonial, are entirely directed to the individual. The evil from which Jesus saves his disciples here and now is, above all, the moral evil of sin and debt which each man has to bear for himself; and that release is not effected by material means, but only by the free and personal will of the living God, and by the faith of those whose sins are forgiven them. The personal religion of the Gospel of Jesus may indeed be summed up in the words: "What doth it profit a man to gain the whole world and lose his own soul?"

BOOK III

THE MYSTERY OF THE PERSON

CHAPTER IX

Jesus and the Messiahship

WHO was Jesus himself, and who did he believe himself to be? These are the last questions that remain: the last and the hardest. For if we have felt some confidence till now that on the whole we were standing on firm ground, in spite of many uncertainties of detail, and in spite of the fact that our reports of the sayings of Jesus are only at second hand, at this point the ground begins to give way beneath our feet. In the reports of our first three Gospels, we shall only be able to distinguish with difficulty, and perhaps often not at all, between what was the belief and conviction of the Christian

Jesus and the Messiahship 167

community on this point, and what was the opinion of Jesus himself. At any rate we have definite proof that here too the faith of his followers gilded and coloured the real image of Jesus. For the point of view from which they painted it was throughout that of faith, and not that of historical accuracy.

All that can be attempted here is to sum up the few fairly well-established conclusions which have been reached as the result of long and laborious investigation. In so doing we must expect to be accused by the one side of accepting too much, and by the other of accepting too little as satisfactorily established. Nevertheless the attempt must be made.

One of these conclusions, which seems now to be definitely assured, in spite of continual discussions in which it is still frequently disputed, is that Jesus considered himself to be the Messiah of his people. For the Gospels this assumption is of course self-evident. But that is not enough to secure the position. Every one of the Messianic utterances of Jesus in our Gospels is disputed on critical grounds, and many of them with good reason. But there is a better starting-point for our contention than any to be obtained by citing individual passages of the tradition. We have certain knowledge that the belief existed from the very beginning among the Christian community that Jesus was Messiah, and, arguing backwards, we can assert that the rise of such a belief would be absolutely inexplicable if Jesus had not declared to his disciples in his lifetime that he was Messiah. It is quite conceivable that the first disciples of Jesus, who by his death and burial had seen all their hopes shattered and their belief in his Messiahship destroyed, might have *returned* to that belief under the influence of their resurrection experiences, if they had formerly possessed it on the ground of the utterances and general conduct of Jesus. But it would be wholly incomprehensible that that belief should have *originated* in their hearts

Jesus and the Messiahship

after the catastrophe, for in that case we must assume that those marvellous experiences of the Easter days produced something completely new in the disciples' souls by a process of sheer magic, and without any psychological preparation. And that we are unable to assume precisely on the ground of our strictly historical point of view.

From such a retrospective survey we conclude, then, that Jesus must have regarded himself in some form or other as the Messiah, and must have imparted that conviction to his disciples. On this assumption we shall have no objections to make against a series of otherwise unimpeachable testimonies of our Gospels to the public assertion by Jesus of his Messianic claims.

It seems then to be established, notwithstanding many arguments which have been urged to the contrary, that at the end of his life Jesus made his entry into Jerusalem as Messiah, that in his public trial before the high priest he solemnly acknowledged himself to be Messiah,[1] and that Pilate caused the words, "This is the King of the Jews," to be inscribed upon his cross. By far the best explanation of the proceedings taken against him is that he was regarded as a false Messiah. It will be recognised more and more clearly as time goes on that the criticism which attempts to shake these well-established points of the tradition merely succeeds in over-reaching itself.

Our Gospel narratives also give us an exceedingly valuable piece of evidence as to when Jesus first spoke of his Messiahship to the disciples. They tell us—probably without themselves realising the profound significance of the event they narrate—that at Cæsarea Philippi, towards the end of his Galilean ministry, Jesus put the question, "Who say ye that I am?" to his disciples, and that Peter answered with the confession, "Thou art the Christ." Jesus thereupon charged them strictly to keep their knowledge to themselves.[2] This

---

[1] For the historical objections to this scene, see above, p. 16. [2] Mark viii. 27.

Jesus and the Messiahship

solemn and significant account can originally—even if the fact was already obscured at the time the Gospels were written—have meant nothing else than that Jesus was here speaking to his disciples for the first time about the secret of his person, and that they on their side acknowledged his Messiahship now for the first time. Moreover we have every right to regard this story as historically trustworthy. It is one of the few narratives of the Synoptists in which the indications of place, and even to a certain extent those of time,[1] are given. It was from the outset so valuable to the community that even the indifferent outward circumstances of time and place were preserved. It relates something which could not possibly have been invented by, and was even opposed to the sense of, the later community. For the latter the Messiahship of Jesus was the surest, most self-evident, and most precious thing

---

[1] The story is connected, at any rate in one direction, by Mark ix. 2 ("after six days") with the transfiguration episode.

about him. How then could he have foreborne to speak of it till towards the end of his life? Wherever the community forged the tradition out of its own consciousness, it naturally made Jesus testify to his Messiahship from the beginning. Witness the consistent representation of the fourth Gospel,[1] and also occasional statements of the first three Evangelists, including Mark, according to which Messianic utterances on Jesus' part already occur at the beginning of his ministry, in contradiction to the scene at Cæsarea Philippi.[2] This paradoxical character of the scene, when compared with the faith of the community, is indeed the best guarantee of its genuineness.[3]

[1] According to the fourth Gospel, John the Baptist is already aware that he is Messiah, as also are the first disciples at their calling: i. 29, 45, 49 ff.

[2] Mark ii. 10, 19 f., 28.

[3] I have not discussed W. Wrede's ingenious repudiation of these views in *Das Messiasgeheimnis in den Evangelien* (1901), because I do not consider his position tenable. The essential point of his argument is that he seeks to discover a consistent tendency in our Gospels

Jesus and the Messiahship 173

But it also confronts us with new problems. Why did Jesus delay so long in speaking of his Messiahship to the disciples? Why did he then charge them so peremptorily to keep it secret? And why did he to all appearance refrain from urging his claims in public until the very end of his life, *i.e.* probably until his entry into Jerusalem? We can scarcely assume that the conviction of his Messiahship only gradually dawned in his own mind towards the end of his life. In days when failure followed hard on failure, when his soul was filled with forebodings of suffering, death and disaster, no room can be found for the growth of such a consciousness. Then all the force of his personality was needed to enable him to cling to the idea, for the Messiahship and suffering, the Messiahship and defeat or even death, were mutually irreconcilable pro-

according to which Jesus intentionally concealed his Messiahship during his lifetime,—a tendency resting perhaps upon the historical fact that Jesus never wished to be Messiah. The best refutation of Wrede is to be found in J. Weiss's *Das älteste Evangelium* (1903).

positions to the ordinary mind. In any case he must already have been sustained by the conviction that he was Messiah by the time he had reached the height of his success. The question as to when it first arose in his mind—whether before or during the course of his ministry—may be left undecided, though it seems to us highly probable that the tradition is right in dating Jesus' awakening to the Messianic consciousness from the moment of his baptism, that is, before the opening of his ministry. For, when we are told that at his baptism by John, Jesus saw in spirit the heavens open and heard a voice crying, "Thou art my son," the original meaning of the passage—although possibly the Evangelists themselves may not have realised its full bearing—was that this was the first awakening of Jesus to the sense that he was the Son of God, or rather the Messiah. Since we can discover no other point in his life at which the Messianic consciousness first made itself felt, we shall provisionally accept the

Jesus and the Messiahship

tradition and assume that the Messianic idea filled his soul from the beginning of his activity, even if it were only in the form of a bold intuition.

But why then this profound and almost timorous reserve? In my opinion the answer to this question lies only in one direction. Jesus himself laboured under an insuperable inward difficulty in the matter. He must have been dominated by a deep and direct sense of the inadequacy of the Messianic title for that which he felt himself by his innermost convictions to be. The Messianic idea was part of the national hopes and the national religion of Israel. The popular expectation was of a heaven-sent king of the line of David, who should come as a mighty ruler, sword in hand, to shatter the Gentile nations, to annihilate Rome, and to set up his universal dominion in Jerusalem, whence he would then rule in wisdom and mercy, filled with the spirit of God, over the righteous and over the prostrate Gentiles. Even when the figure of this king was painted in supernatural colours, and the Messiah was no longer expected as the Son of David, but as a miraculous apparition descending from heaven, the Judge of the world clothed in God-like majesty, he still remained the national king who was to destroy the Gentiles. It is easy to see how foreign this figure, glowing with the passions of national fanaticism, must have been to the whole nature and being of Jesus, and how far from Messianic in this sense was his life and work. Just as the popular ideas of the Kingdom of God and of the Judgment were found inadequate, when closely examined, as expressions of the message which Jesus brought, so the Messianic title was inadequate and even dangerous as an expression of the true character of his personality. While Jesus could still speak freely of the Kingdom of God and of the Judgment, and could pour the new wine into the old skins, he found himself in an altogether different position in adopting the title of Messiah. The Kingdom

Jesus and the Messiahship 177

and the Judgment were still things of the future. But from the moment that Jesus publicly assumed the name of Messiah, he turned the future into the present, and, as indeed history has shown, ushered in the decisive final hour. The objection that under these conditions Jesus might have adopted a better method than mere silence, by instructing his hearers openly in the manner in which he wished his Messiahship understood, shows a failure to appreciate the inward delicacy and tenderness of his perplexed self-consciousness, and, above all, the volcanic nature of the ground on which he stood. An open claim to the Messiahship on Jesus' part would have brought all the explosive material which had gradually been fermenting in the hearts of the expectant people to the point of combustion, and must have banded his opponents together in deadly enmity to his pretensions. And when once the fanatic spirit of the mob was roused on one side or the other, who could have arrested its mad career?

This view, however, is certainly open to one objection. Why did Jesus associate himself at all with Messianic hopes which were so foreign to his inmost being; why did he not shun them altogether? The answer is that in another direction they were absolutely necessary to him. Just as he could not dispense with the ideas of the Kingdom and the Judgment if he wished to make himself intelligible to his countrymen, so he could not dispense with the Messianic idea if he wished to be intelligible to himself. One thing that stands out in the personality of Jesus is the fact that he wished to be more than a mere member of a band, even if the band were that of the prophets. He felt himself irresistibly drawn towards the extraordinary and the unique. And, as we know, he announced the approach of the Kingdom of Heaven. According to the popular ideal, however, this was inconceivable without the Messiah, and thus he found his position decided for him. For he could not be content

Jesus and the Messiahship 179

with the rôle of a forerunner. He felt that he stood in such closeness of communion with God the Father as belonged to none before or after him. He was conscious of speaking the last and decisive word; he felt that what he did was final and that no one would come after him. The certainty and simple force of his work, the sunshine, clearness, and freshness of his whole attitude rest upon this foundation. We cannot eliminate from his personality without destroying it the trait of super-prophetic consciousness, the consciousness of the accomplisher to whose person the flight of the ages and the whole destiny of his followers is linked. And when Jesus wished to give form and expression to this consciousness, and thereby to lift it from its state of fermentation into one of clearness and stability, the only possibility that presented itself to him was that of the Messianic idea,—of that figure of the kingly consummator standing at the end of time, as popular imagination had painted it with its earthly colours.

Thus the Messianic idea was the only possible form in which Jesus could clothe his inner consciousness, and yet an inadequate form; it was a necessity, but also a heavy burden which he bore in silence almost to the end of his life; it was a conviction which he could never enjoy with a whole heart.

CHAPTER X

The Son of Man

THE difficulties with which Jesus was forced to contend will become still plainer when we consider the particular forms in which his Messianic consciousness expressed itself. As we have already indicated, the nature of the Messianic hopes at the time of Jesus varied enormously, oscillating between the poles of a purely earthly and a supernatural conception. Thus the best answer to the question, what exact image Jesus formed in his own mind of his Messiahship, will be found by turning our attention to the Messianic titles and attributes which he was wont to confer upon himself. Yet in reality there is only one such title which enters seriously into consideration. He practically deprecated the name "Son of David," which expressed the more earthly side of the Messianic hopes,[1] although he may occasionally have allowed it, as the tradition states, from the mouth of a third person.[2] Nor did he use the more general title "Son of God," which has its origin in certain words of the Old Testament, as a title proper. The heavenly voice at his baptism, says the tradition, cried "Thou art my son," and Jesus answered the high priest's question, "Art thou the Son of God?" in the affirmative.[3] But when he himself rejoices that "no one knoweth the Son, save the Father; neither doth any know the Father, save the Son, and

[1] The meaning of Mark xii. 35 ff. is a denial of the idea that the Messiah must be the Son of David.

[2] Mark x. 47; xi. 10.

[3] It may be well to emphasise the fact that in the time and *milieu* of Jesus the term "Son of God" meant simply "God's chosen one," *i.e.* the Messiah. It should never be connected (as it still is so often by the orthodox mind) with the dogmas of the miraculous birth and the Eternal Son, even though the title may already have borne a deeper meaning in the eyes of our Evangelists, who were writing from the standpoint of the Christian community.

The Son of Man

he to whom the Son willeth to reveal him,"[1] the antithesis between Father and Son here shows that the word "Son" is not meant in the sense of a title. No, according to the tradition of our Gospels there is but one title—though that one is of the utmost importance—which Jesus certainly applied to himself: that of the *Son of Man*. In a large number of passages Jesus speaks of himself in the third person as the "Son of Man."

This term places us again before a difficult and far-reaching problem, to which, especially in recent times, an immense amount of labour has been devoted. We shall again endeavour to present our readers with the conclusions which have to some extent been established and accepted. Two pretty generally recognised principles will serve as starting-points. First, it is now admitted by the majority of scholars that the designation "Son of Man" is a true Messianic *title*. Almost everywhere that Jesus calls himself the Son of Man in our

[1] Matt. xi. 27.

Synoptic tradition there follows some saying which refers to his specifically Messianic dignity, or at least to the unique position and destiny of his person.[1] Thus it occurs in connection with utterances about his future coming in glory to judge the world, or about the miraculous powers which he was already exercising upon earth; and in contrast to this we are told that the Son of Man must suffer and die and must for the present live in lowliness. Always, however, the title serves to emphasise something extraordinary, something that applies only to his own person in its peculiar calling. The second principle, on the other hand, is that, etymologically speaking, the title "Son of Man," as spoken in Aramaic, means neither more nor less than the word "Man." It was impossible to make any distinction between the phrases "Son of Man" and "Man" in the Aramaic dialect, so that it is quite possible that in occasional

---

[1] See esp. Mark ii. 10, 28; viii. 31, 38; ix. 9, 12, 31; x. 33, 45; xiii. 26 f.; xiv. 62.

passages where this title appears in our Gospels, Jesus did not intend to speak of himself as the Son of Man, but only of man in general.[1] It is indeed only from the sense and emphasis of any given saying that the difference can be ascertained.

If, however, the term "Son of Man" is held on the one hand to be a Messianic title, and on the other is found to be synonymous with the colourless word "man," we must conclude that, if Jesus did apply this designation to himself, he was merely adopting thereby a previously coined Messianic term, which was already endowed with a special meaning. The most ordinary word can, when used terminologically, acquire a special meaning which does not belong to it intrinsically, but is as it were arbitrarily bound up with it. We shall now have to inquire, therefore, whether the Judaism of that day was not already acquainted with a title of "the Man" for the Messiah, and further,

[1] One of the obvious instances is Mark ii. 28 (and possibly ii. 10).

what ideas it embodied in that title. And in effect we find that the literature of later Judaism yields the answer to the riddle. In some of these writings the coming Messiah is spoken of as "one like unto a man," or even simply as "the Man." The expression occurs with particular frequency in the so-called Similitudes of the Book of Enoch, a decidedly Jewish document of the middle of the first century A.D. But above all the famous passage in Daniel (vii. 13) —"And behold, there came with the clouds of heaven one like unto a son of man . . . and there was given him dominion and glory and a kingdom"—was generally interpreted as early as the time of Jesus as referring to the personal Messiah, although the author of the Book of Daniel himself perhaps only wished it to be understood as a symbol of the people of Israel. In short, the title "Man" or "Son of Man" for the Messiah was already in existence.

How it arose and what it originally meant we need not here trouble ourselves to inquire. Jesus himself did not inquire, but merely took over the title as he found it. It is, however, of interest to note that this title represents a perfectly definite conception of the Messiah. This Messianic Man is no longer the earthly king of the line of David, as popular imagination painted him; he is a supernatural figure, he comes down from heaven, he was with God from the beginning of the world, he appears in the splendour of his divine glory, and he is actually the Judge of the world, thus displacing God Himself from that position. In adopting this title, therefore, Jesus had a purpose in view; by its use he could define his Messianic claims more narrowly and could brush aside the coarser popular and national ideas of the Messiah as the Son of David; he could in fact set up his claim to be Messiah in the supernatural sense of the Son of Man.

Here we must pause to consider certain critical objections which have recently been urged with ever-increasing force, and are indeed partially justified. Many critics have expressed the view that Jesus never did adopt the title

"Son of Man," and that it merely represents the later tradition of the community. Where Jesus simply spoke in the first person, they consider that the Christian tradition interpolated the title "Son of Man." It is not unjustly argued that this continual speaking in the third person seems unnatural in the mouth of Jesus, and inconsistent with the plainness and simplicity of his speech in other respects. More than this, it is pointed out that a comparison between our first three Gospels actually proves that in many places the title "Son of Man" was inserted by the later Evangelist, where originally there had only stood the word "I."[1] Finally, it has been asked how it was possible to ascribe to a human being living the ordinary life of man on earth these apparently fantastic claims to the dignity of the Son of Man. For it must not be forgotten that the Jewish conception of the Man-Messiah embraced within itself the claims to

---

[1] One of the best examples is afforded by Matt. xvi. 13 as compared with Mark viii. 27.

pre-existence and the judgeship of the world, whereas, according to the surest tradition of our earliest Gospels, it never occurred to Jesus to attribute a primæval existence to himself, and whereas we have good reason to assert, as we shall see below, that Jesus never made any claim to be the future Judge of the world, although our first three Gospels, following the belief of the community, certainly represent him as making it.

These objections are partially right, and in face of them we shall only be able to maintain the assertion that Jesus did call himself the Son of Man with certain reservations.

We must in fact go a little further back in order to obtain a clearer view. Our Gospel tradition itself will set us on the right road, albeit not without some contradictions and inconsistencies. Roughly speaking, then, it may be said that it places the utterances about the Son of Man towards the end of the life of Jesus.[1] And it shows us with unmistakable

[1] See the passages in Mark cited above, p. 184.

clearness that the idea of the Son of Man was intimately connected in his mind with the dawning conviction of suffering and death. The sayings about the return of the Son of Man in glory are balanced with remarkable closeness by the prophecies that he must suffer and die.[1] It is true that the gravest critical objections have been raised against these prophecies. It has been argued that they appear in a very monotonous way, and that they are in reality no more than a greatly abridged account of the Passion given in prophetic form. Nothing would have been more natural and more conceivable than that the Christian community should not have tolerated the idea that death overtook their Lord unawares, and should therefore have put into his mouth detailed prophecies as to his future destiny. One fragment of the tradition, however, forms an impassable barrier to these contentions—the scene of Gethsemane, which no follower could have invented, and which bears

[1] Mark viii. 31 (38); ix. 9, 12, 31; x. 33.

within itself the stamp of genuine history. That scene shows that Jesus was not surprised by his fate, but on the contrary that he went to meet it with a full and complete consciousness of what lay before him. Here we have no longer a mere vague foreboding, but knowledge reaching almost to the point of certainty. From the scene of Gethsemane, however, we can argue backwards. Such a clear vision of his fate and such resignation to the Will of God can only have been won gradually by sharp inward conflict. Stronger and stronger forebodings must have invaded his soul long before Gethsemane. Nor indeed could it have been otherwise. As the non-success of his efforts among his own people became more and more evident, as the conviction grew that that people was hastening along the road to destruction, rejected of God, so the goal of his own life must have grown darker and darker, and the presentiment ever stronger that his labours would end in calamity. It is quite possible and even probable that Jesus spoke to his disciples during his last days in Galilee of his dark and bitter forebodings. If, as must be admitted, the Gospel tradition has obliterated almost every individual and convincing touch from its monotonously repeated prophecies, there are still a few passages in which some piece of original and uninventable tradition lingers.[1] But however that may be, it is enough for us to know that we have good reasons for upholding the historical truth of the prophecies of suffering and death.

And herewith we shall arrive at a final understanding of Jesus' conceptions, or, let us say, his auguries, concerning the Son of Man. It is in this connection that they find their true place. In face of the threatening doom of final failure, Jesus clung fast to the Danielic prophecy of the Son of Man, and applied it to himself. The form in which, with death and failure before his eyes, he still maintained his faith in his cause and in his God, was to declare to himself, his friends, and his foes that

[1] Mark viii. 31 f.; x. 32.

after his death he would return in glory as the Son of Man upon the clouds of heaven.

This gives us the necessary limitations within which it is possible to maintain the use by Jesus of the title "Son of Man"; and with them the objections raised above disappear of their own accord. The title "Son of Man" cannot have been used as a regular and constant self-designation by Jesus. Not until the end of his life, and then only briefly and sparingly, did he adopt the name. Probably he did not speak of his hopes in that respect with any greater certainty, but rather in the same dark, allusive, and foreboding terms as he employed when speaking of his death, his sufferings, or his failure.

The stereotyped way in which the Synoptists represent Jesus as using the title "Son of Man" is not historical. There speaks, not the earthly Jesus, but the dogmatic conviction of his followers. Yet this constantly repeated use of the title by the tradition is best explained on the supposition that it is based on a few genuine words of Jesus, while the fact that the mysterious title never appears in the narrative part of the Gospels, but always in the sayings of Jesus, would otherwise have no explanation. The process by which it gradually spread from these few passages of genuine tradition into so many of the words of Jesus would then be partially revealed by the Gospels themselves. Nor can we regard his own use of the title as artificial, when we consider that it was only at rare moments of the deepest emotion, when the super-earthly figure of the Messiah rose before his soul like a new and strange apparition, that he spoke of himself in these terms. Finally, if Jesus only caught at the idea of the Son of Man in this semi-prophetic way, it would be easy to understand why he did not adopt its full content, including the ideas of pre-existence and of his own Judgeship of the world; to him the idea of the Son of Man meant only one thing his return in glory.

CHAPTER XI

Conclusion

TORTUOUS paths are these that we have tried to follow in the soul-life of Jesus, and hence it is but dimly and uncertainly that we have been able to trace them. One thing only stands out still more clearly than before— how insufficient and even dangerous to the true being of Jesus were these Messianic ideas. The expectation at which his broodings finally landed him, that he would return in the immediate future upon the clouds of heaven, surrounded by his angels— how foreign it sounds to us! History itself, with its irrevocably different course, has stepped in here, sifting and winnowing.

And yet we must not forget that behind

this transient form a lofty and eternal truth lies hidden. The idea of the Son of Man was the outward means by which Jesus rose superior to his fate, and enabled himself, and above all his disciples, to hold fast to their faith in his person and his cause even beyond the grave. This adoption of the idea of suffering and death side by side with his personal conviction—which still remained unshaken—that he was called and sent by God, was a truly immense achievement, precisely because the form in which he held the conviction of his divine mission was that of the Messianic consciousness. There was something horrible and unheard-of about the idea of a suffering and dying Messiah to the minds of Jesus' contemporaries. Nor could he find it expressed anywhere in the Old Testament. No one in all the centuries gone by had found it there; nor could it have been taken thence, for the simple reason that the Old Testament did not contain it. It was only through their faith in the Crucified

Conclusion 197

One that his followers afterwards read it into the fifty-third chapter of Isaiah.[1] No, Jesus was left to face the dark ways of God and an enormous task alone. He had so to ennoble and to transfigure suffering and failure, the abominations of Judaism, that they could become the crown of all that his followers believed of their Messiah. He had to conquer a new world which was closed to Israel, but within which Paul, the quondam Jew, could exultingly cry a generation later, " We rejoice in our sufferings " ; which Goethe meant when he spoke of the sanctity of sorrow revealed by Christianity. Jesus accomplished the task partially by means of the idea of the Son of Man. You cannot make an omelette without breaking eggs. Yet this idea of a swiftly approaching outward glory was not the factor which rendered possible, but only facilitated, his bold act of

---

[1] This chapter is, at any rate in its orignal sense, not Messianic, however various the interpretations which it now permits.

faith. The foundation of his new thoughts and convictions lay deeper, in the relations of personal trust between himself and his Father. Because Jesus accepted his destiny as coming direct from the hand of God, because he went the dark way in the spirit of the Psalmist— " Nevertheless will I remain with thee, and thou holdest me with thy right hand,"— therefore he rose above his fate, therefore he could wed the thought of death with the conviction that he was in a peculiar sense God's envoy. Not in his utterances about the Son of Man, but in Gethsemane do the calm, deep grandeur and the sure foundation of his life reveal themselves.

The same holds good of the whole Messianic consciousness of Jesus; it was the form in which an eternal meaning clothed itself. We have already shown why the title of Messiah was necessary to Jesus in its general aspect, apart from certain details: because it alone coincided with his consciousness of his own unique position and super-prophetic significance. Let us contemplate for a moment this sovereign sense of leadership by which Jesus was possessed, and the inimitable sureness with which it unfolded itself in every direction. He knew how to value the authorities of the past, but he placed himself above them. He was of more account than kings and prophets, than David, Solomon, and the Temple.[1] The tradition of the elders he met with his "But I say unto you," and even Moses was not an authority to whom he gave unqualified submission. As with the past, so too the present bowed before him. John the Baptist he thought the greatest among the sons of men, yet it was not Jesus who put the question, "Art thou he that cometh?" to John, but John to Jesus, and he answered the inquiry with a veiled though yet distinct affirmative. In a time of confusion and perplexity and of the appearance of many false Messiahs, his own confidence reared itself proudly and boldly: "None knoweth the Son,

[1] Luke x. 23 f.; Matt. xii. 6, 41 f.; Mark ii. 25 f.

save the Father; neither doth any know the Father, save the Son."[1] He possessed the simple greatness that won the hearts of the simple men and women of the people.[2] Wherever he showed himself his person inspired unlimited trust and lofty enthusiasm, and a faith which made the impossible easy and lifted him and his surroundings into an unfamiliar wonder-world. In controversy he was a rock of strength. His hottest and noblest wrath was united with the serenest calm. He was invulnerable in dispute and ever victorious. Whom he attacked he branded for all eternity; what he respected he made eternally precious. He turned the word Pharisee into a term of reproach, and exalted the despised Samaritan. The outcast and rejected he raised with his wonderful power and set them on firm ground. He could venture into a world full of dirt and evil repute because he himself was strong and pure and free. He riveted his disciples to himself as no one before or

[1] Matt. xi. 27.   [2] Luke xi. 27 f.; xiv. 15 f.; xix. 1 f.

Conclusion   201

since has ever riveted his followers. He set them the alternative of all or nothing, and they obeyed: "Master, we have left all for thy sake."[1] He allowed no looking back, no consideration even for the strongest claims of piety. He had higher tasks to set them. He could dare to say, "If any man cometh unto me, and hateth not his own father and mother and wife and children and brethren and sisters, yea, and his own life also, he cannot be my disciple."[2] In the days of failure and dark foreboding he tightened the bonds between himself and his disciples still more closely. He demanded of them a never-ceasing faithfulness down to death itself, and a steadfast affirmation of his cause and his person. "Everyone who shall confess me before men, him will I also confess before my Father which is in heaven."[3] Such words either come from thoughtless presumption or from the very highest strength and confidence. History has decided for the latter.

[1] Mark x. 28.   [2] Luke xiv. 26.   [3] Matt. x. 32.

Yet with all this—and here we touch the culminating point—he never overstepped the limits of the purely human. The almighty God remained before his eyes a sublime and lofty presence; he did not presume to place himself at His side. When he riveted his disciples' souls to his own, he did so because he wished to lead them on and beyond to the living God. He wished to be the way to the heavenly Father, not the goal itself. He drew a sharp dividing line between God and himself. "None is good save one, even God," he said, so placing himself on the side of struggling humanity.[1] He came to the baptism of repentance and forgiveness of sins as given by the Baptist. To the woman out of the multitude who pressed her impetuous homage upon him, he answered: "Yea, rather, blessed are they that hear the word of *God*, and keep it."[2] "Whosoever shall do the will of *God*," he cried, "the same is my brother and sister and mother."[3] He never demanded faith in

[1] Mark x. 18. [2] Luke xi. 28. [3] Mark iii. 35.

Conclusion 203

himself as he demanded faith in God. In all his parables—the most genuine part of his sayings that we possess—he places man in direct relation with the living God, while he himself retires completely into the background.

Nevertheless, in appropriating the idea of the Son of Man, he seems almost to overstep the boundary. Yet he did not thereby place himself on a level with God. Above all he did not lay claim to the Judgeship of the world, although that conception was, strictly speaking, included in that of the Son of Man. It is true that in the narratives of our Gospels the opposite seems to be the case. But it is inconceivable that Jesus, who stamped the fear of that almighty God who had power to damn body and soul together upon the hearts of his disciples with such marvellous energy,[1] and who could speak of that fear because he shared it to the bottom of his soul, should now have arrogated to himself the Judgeship of the world in the place of God. This is

[1] See above, pp. 110 f.

an instance of the faith of the community working upon the tradition. The progressive development of a single saying which is reported in five passages of our Gospels may serve to make this clear. Matthew alone gives the primitive version: "Everyone who shall confess me before men, him will I also confess before my Father which is in heaven. But whosoever shall deny me before men, him will I also deny before my Father which is in heaven."[1] Mark already modifies the saying thus: "Whosoever shall be ashamed of me and of my words . . . the Son of man[2] also shall be ashamed of him, when he cometh *in the glory of his Father* with the holy angels."[3] And finally, in the passage corresponding to Mark's, Matthew[4] has the still more comprehensive utterance: "For the Son of man shall

---

[1] Matt. x. 32.

[2] Observe here also the encroachment of the title "Son of Man."

[3] Mark viii. 38.

[4] The first-quoted saying of Matthew belongs to the so-called Logia document.

come in the glory of his Father with his angels; and then shall he render unto every man according to his deeds."[1] Thus as the tradition was handed down by his community, Jesus was gradually removed from the position of a simple witness for his followers before God's tribunal to that of the actual Judge of the world. Supported by this piece of evidence, we shall be justified in holding all those passages in which Jesus appears as the Judge of mankind to be the dogmatism of the Christian community and not the opinion of Jesus himself.

Finally, this most human picture is crowned by suffering and death. We have already seen how Jesus rose above his fate by his infinite trust in a heavenly Father, and how he fused the idea of suffering into his Messianic consciousness. But here the question arises, whether he also assigned any special purpose and significance to his death. We can no

[1] Matt. xvi. 27, and besides the above-quoted passages, the same saying occurs in Luke viii. 25 and xii. 8 f.

longer decide this question with any certainty. Practically only two passages in our Gospel tradition need be considered with regard to it: first, the saying that the Son of Man came to give his life a ransom for many,[1] and secondly, the institution of the Last Supper. In the present state of our knowledge, however, we shall unfortunately be obliged to give up all hope of ascertaining the original meaning of the Last Supper. In any case, a justifiable and widespread doubt has again been raised in recent times as to whether that solemn action of Jesus at his last meal with the disciples had anything directly to do with the thought of his death. Only one thing is probably certain, that at the original Supper Jesus did not mean to institute a sacrament in the Catholic, Lutheran, or Calvinistic sense. The Last Supper may therefore be left out of account for our present purpose, and thus only a single saying (Mark x. 45) remains to be considered. But in view of the nature of our tradition it

[1] Mark x. 45.

is impossible to construct anything upon an isolated saying of this sort. It is also improbable on general grounds that Jesus should have asked himself the purpose of his suffering and death at all, if, as we believe, his thoughts about his future destiny remained doubtful and perplexed until the hour of Gethsemane. It is certainly possible that he interpreted his death dimly and prophetically as a ransom for many. As the Jewish tradition made the martyr-brothers of the Maccabean rising repeatedly express in their prayers the thought that their unmerited suffering must appease the wrath of God against his people, so Jesus may also have caught at this idea and have expressed the hope that through his suffering the wrath of God against the multitude (of Israel) might be appeased. And indeed a deep and eternal truth lies hidden in this faith in the vicarious suffering of the righteous and the infinite value of martyrdom. But we can no longer see clearly in this matter. One thing only is certain, that Jesus never conceived or expressed the thought that God's forgiveness of sins depended absolutely upon his own sacrificial death or upon the vicarious atonement rendered by his death. The parable of the Prodigal Son and the unqualified certainty with which he constantly proclaimed the omnipresent, merciful, and sin-forgiving God emphatically protest against such a view.

The Christian Church, in brooding over the death of her Lord, has continued throughout the centuries to seek some special purpose in it, lying outside the mere bodily death of Jesus. In her, that is to say in Paul, whose spirit gave the direction to centuries of development, the Jewish feeling that suffering and defeat were shameful, ignominious, and abhorrent, a problem which demanded special explanation, continued to operate in this one particular. I believe that we shall be nearer to the spirit of Jesus if we wholly abandon these specialised views of his death. For us his suffering, crucifixion, and death are the crown and consummation of his life. We cannot

Conclusion

conceive any ending to the life of Jesus grander, more powerful, or even other than it actually was. The cross and the crown of thorns do but complete his figure, and lift it far above those of the other founders of religions. Only by walking the appointed path of sorrow in silence and simplicity, without pretension and without faltering, in undiminished trust in his heavenly Father, in the unbroken conviction of his own divine mission, did he render his highest service. Only so did he reveal the new moral world, ennoble suffering and defeat, and create the "worship of sorrow" and the faith in the eternal value of martyrdom. Only here did he reach his consummation as leader of the ages and nations to God.

Leader of the ages and nations to God,— for death and the grave could not hold his person and his spirit. The days of the Passion were followed by Easter in the disciples' hearts, and with the tidings that their Lord had risen again and was alive they founded the first Christian community. What the disciples actually experienced in those Easter days belongs not to an account of Jesus' life and personality, but to the history of the primitive Church. One thing, however, must be said in conclusion of this brief sketch, in order that we may judge the life of Jesus by the proper standard. The manner in which they experienced these impressions belongs to the outward and passing form. But the inmost substance of their Easter visions was that the figure of their Lord and Master appeared again before their mental eyes, clad in all the strength and splendour in which they had known it upon earth, yet now transfigured and freed from the chances and changes of our mortal life. It was that figure itself, and no experience of an outward nature, that compelled their souls, when they declared that their Lord lived again and would be with them alway, even unto the end of the world.

To this the history of man has said Yea

and Amen. And in spite of the separation of time and the frequently exasperating uncertainty of the tradition, we who occupy our place in the history of Jesus through the centuries can still feel his presence near us, with his trust in God and his nearness to God, his relentless moral earnestness, his conquest of pain, his certainty of the forgiveness of sins, and his eternal hope.

And when we absorb ourselves in the contemplation of that figure we feel a great uprising of the spirit. For there we touch indeed upon the foundations of our own spiritual and personal existence.

PRINTED BY NEILL AND CO., LTD., EDINBURGH.

www.ingramcontent.com/pod-product-compliance
Lightning Source LLC
Chambersburg PA
CBHW070740160426
43192CB00009B/1510